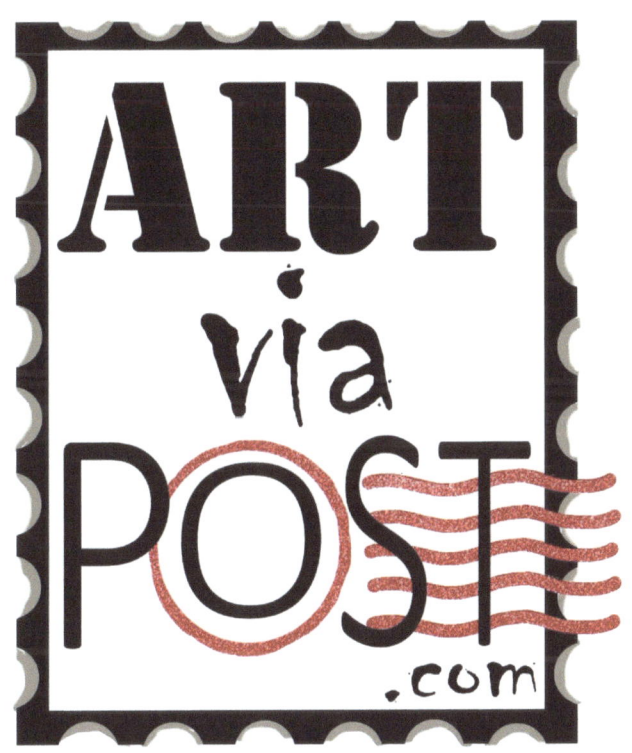

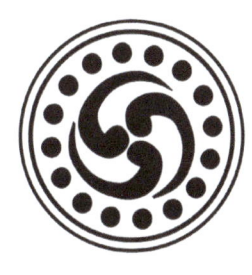

WHITE DHARMA LTD.

Dedication

To the incredible group of mail artists from around the globe who create without fear of judgment and send their art into the interlinking web of postal systems worldwide. These artists do so as a form of creativity, collaboration and friendship. They ask for nothing in return, the mail is a gift. It is to these artists that send their thoughts, their hopes, their dreams, their creations, their Art, via post that we dedicate this book.

A Note:

We tried our best to read the handwriting of the artists on the envelopes we received. If we misspelled your name or contact information, please let us know so that we can correct it for future printings.

Mail Art and Correspondence Art

Don't be deceived. Mail art and correspondence art have been around for over 40 years. This underground art phenomenon has amazing history and is written about in books, journals, articles and numerous websites.

Beyond the brightly colored images of some mail artists you will find a complex, prolific network of individuals who not only voice their opinions on a broad range of topics from social, political, environmental, and counter-culture issues to scientific and artistic collaborations; all on an envelope's exterior and boldly inside.

There is no right or wrong way to be a mail artist. You don't need to have agendas, art degrees or formal training. You only need an envelope or postcard to convey your hand embellished message, a recipient and a stamp. Some use mail art as their form of artistic expression, others for relaxation.

Art Via Post opened a call to artists of all types asking them to use an envelope as their canvas. There was no pre-determined topic; the message was up to the sender. This book is meant to be a visual experience combining a myriad of different artists from all around the globe who sent their work to us. We don't judge their style, talent or message. We experience the envelope as the gift it is: A special piece of mail that was hand done, carefully considered, executed and dropped in the post box.

We encourage you explore mail art. To join some of the more robust online platforms that will allow you to hone your skills and sharpen your mind (IUOMA.org for starts). Or, simply peruse this book and enjoy the envelopes for what they are - Art. Perhaps you, too, will be inspired to send someone Art Via Post.

Denise D. Price
Emma Scott

Denise D. Price

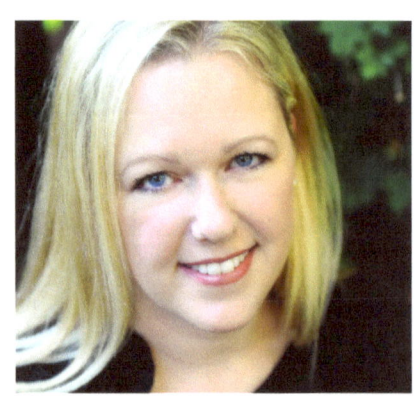

Denise D. Price is a self-taught paper engineer and illustrator and loves paper. She was introduced to the paper arts over twenty years ago during the first year the Clayton College for Boys opened to girls. She attended, by invitation and scholarship, a summer arts intensive. It was at that Institute that her passion for the arts was stoked and has burned ever since. She holds an MBA in International Business and is a chronic entrepreneur. In her free time, she has trained in paper arts with some of the finest traveling pop-up professors in the world at the historic Bennett Street School in Boston and Massachusetts College of Art and Design.

Much of what makes its way onto Denise's pages are influenced by her global travels. Having seen twenty countries on five continents, her art is a combination of ephemera, design and artistic expression and echoes images and experiences from her travels. She lives in Cambridge, Massachusetts where she daydreams of her home at the base of the Rocky Mountains and how to make paper into things that delight and transport the viewer to a parallel plane of the same universe. Denise's debut printed creation is the Freedom Trail Pop Up Book of Boston published by White Dharma and is Boston's first pop up book.

Emma Scott

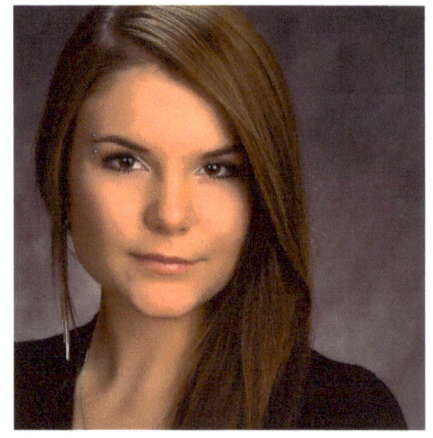

Emma Scott has studied many forms of art including jewelry and metal works, printmaking, painting and drawing, ceramics, life drawing, clothing design & construction, manipulating glass, and mixed media sculpture. She has studied and had her work displayed at Massachusetts College of Art and Design as well as Pratt Institute in New York. She is also a strong supporter of mail art and all artists. Ms. Scott was born in Cambridge, Massachusetts and though she resides in Lexington, her roots have remained strong in Cambridge and Boston. Supporting her community, her fellow artists as well as nourishing her own passions, art is what Emma lives to do. She thrives on new experiences and creativity.

Exhibition Location

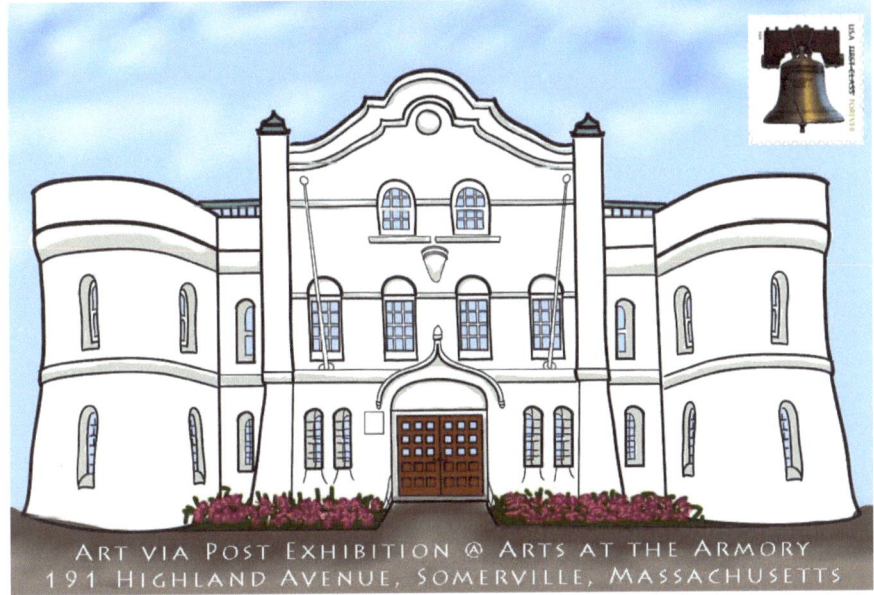

ART VIA POST EXHIBITION @ ARTS AT THE ARMORY
191 HIGHLAND AVENUE, SOMERVILLE, MASSACHUSETTS

The Art Via Post Exhibition was held at the Arts at the Armory in Somerville, Massaschusetts in February of 2015.

The Armory was built in 1903 by George A. Moore to house the Somerville Light Infantry of the Massachusetts Volunteer Militia. For nearly seventy years after that, it also housed the Massachusetts National Guard. For the last thirty years, the building was used for some community events but largely sat vacant until the State of Massachusetts decided to sell the building in 2004.

The historic armory was purchased by Joseph and Nabil Sater, in collaboration with Highland Realty Trust, in April 2004 from the Commonwealth of Massachusetts. Owners of the famous Middle East music club in Central Square, Cambridge and patrons of the arts, the Sater brothers successfully embarked upon a vision to create a community arts center for the City of Somerville. Joined later by partner, Alan Carrier, they contracted with Single Speed Design who served as award winning architects for the project.

Since 2004, the Armory has been completely restored and brought up to code. Many of the Armory's historic elements have been preserved. Art Via Post was pleased to have the opportunity to exhibit the envelopes in the very busy Armory where they were viewed by many people in the Armory's Café. Art Via Post would like to express sincere thanks to the hard working staff at the Arts for the Armory and the Sater brothers for their support.

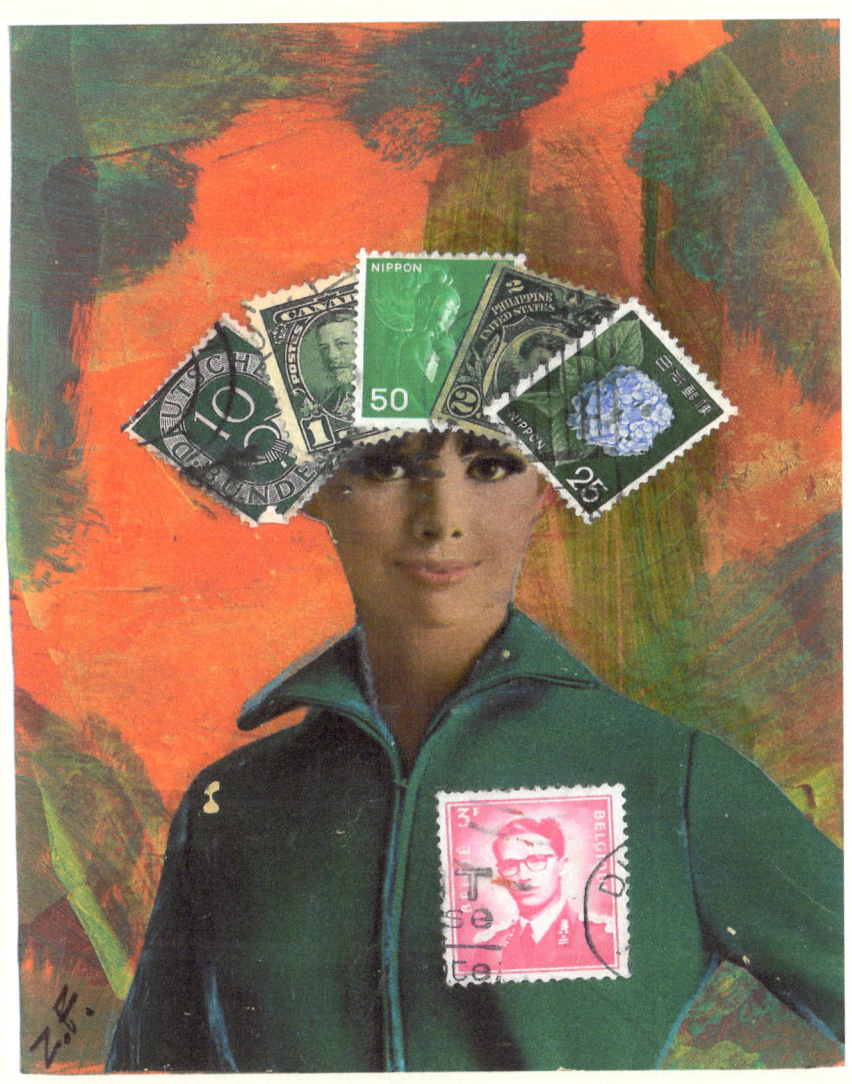

"I love creating mailart because it's a piece of art that in many ways shows the recipient that they were really thought of. I make it a rule to never tell someone I've sent them something nor do I ever ask if they've received it. I truly love the element of suprise. When I photograph each piece, I prefer to let it be the star, one piece at a time. To me, it makes it so much a piece of art instead of a piece of mail." - Zeeflower

PALCZEWSKI, GLORIA
AKA ZEEFLOWER

Los Angeles, California

Instagram: Zeeflower

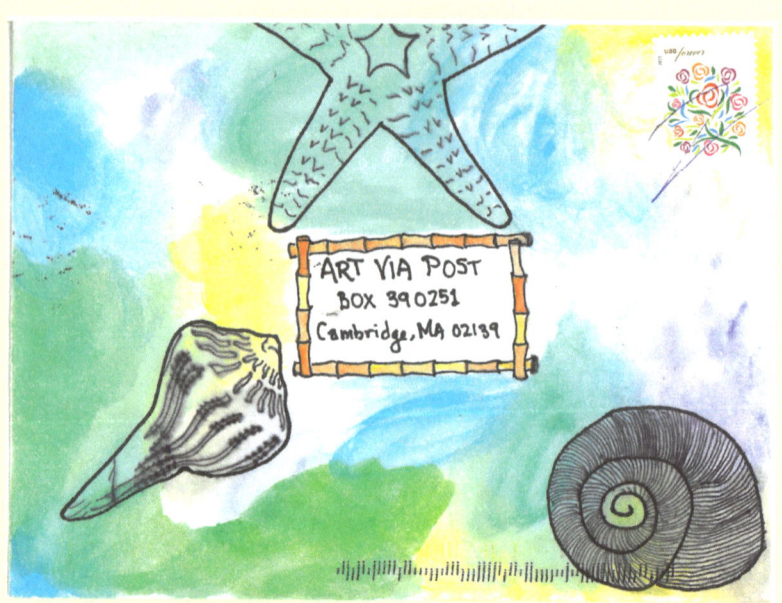

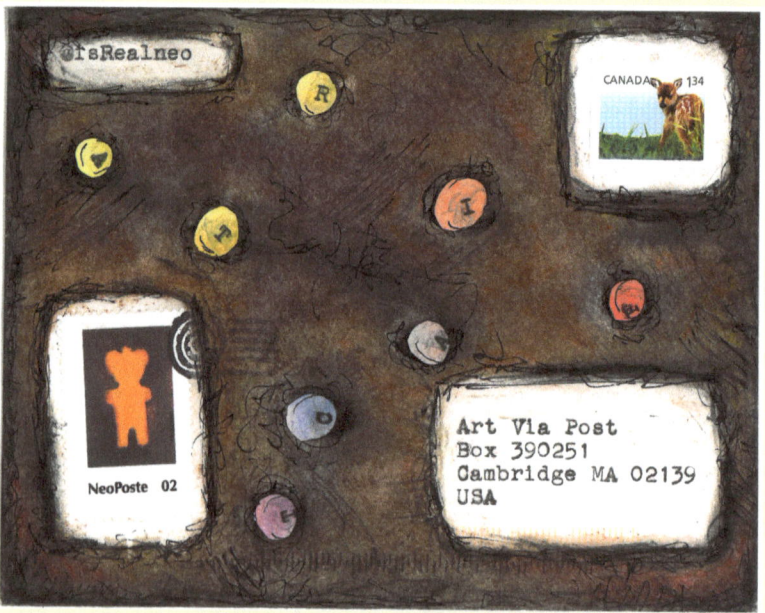

HOM, LAUREN

Chicago, Illinois

REALNEO

Ontario, Canada

realneo.com

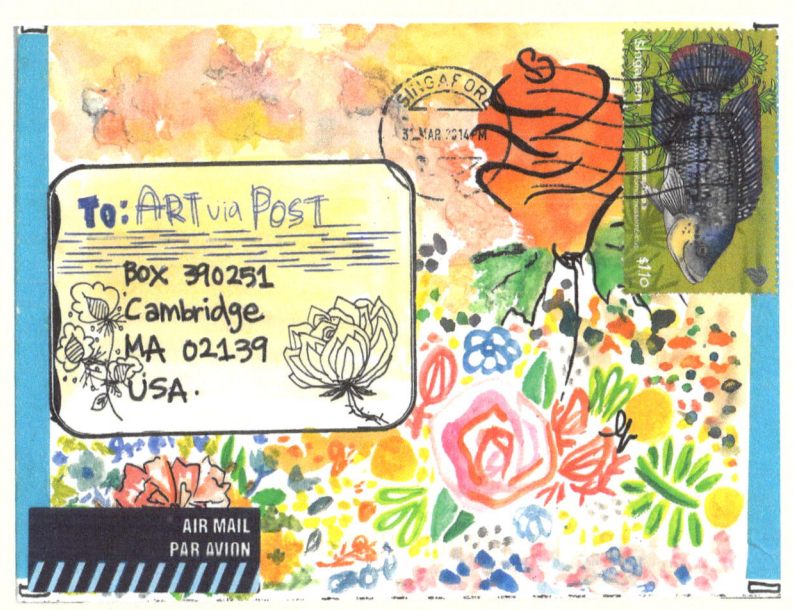

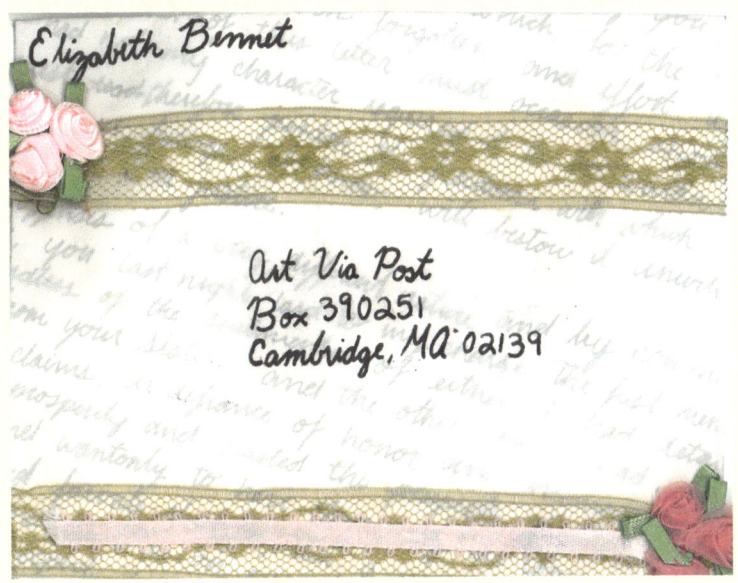

RUTH

Singapore

TUCKER, KAYLEE

Highland Park, Illinoic

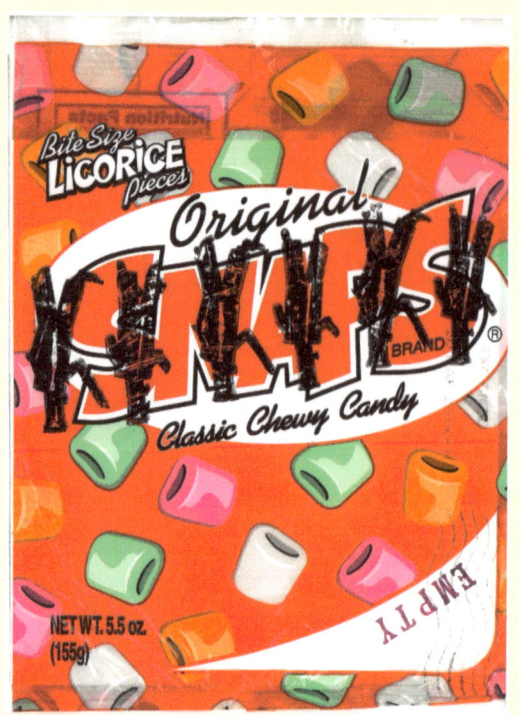

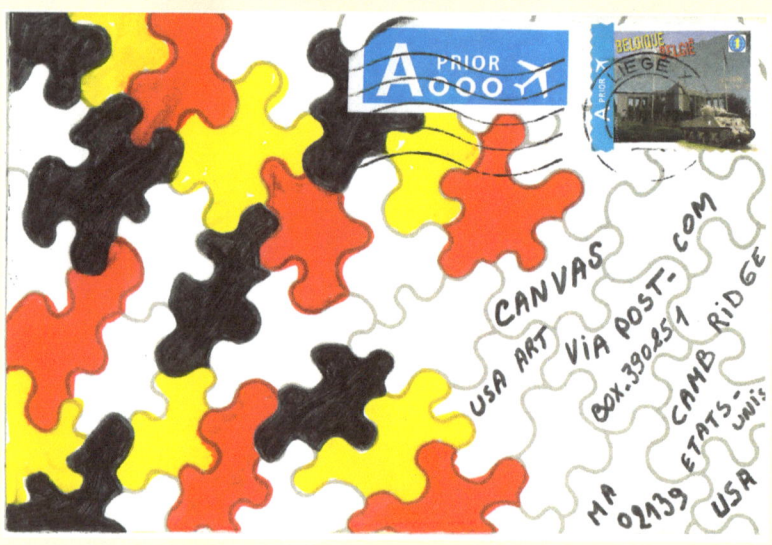

JEAN, CONNIE

Cocoa Beach, Florida

FABIENNE, GONAY

Belgium

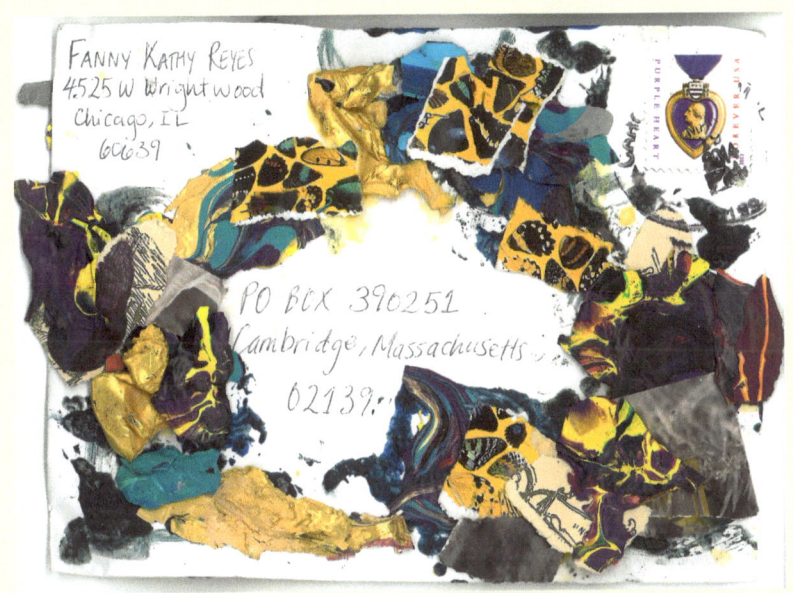

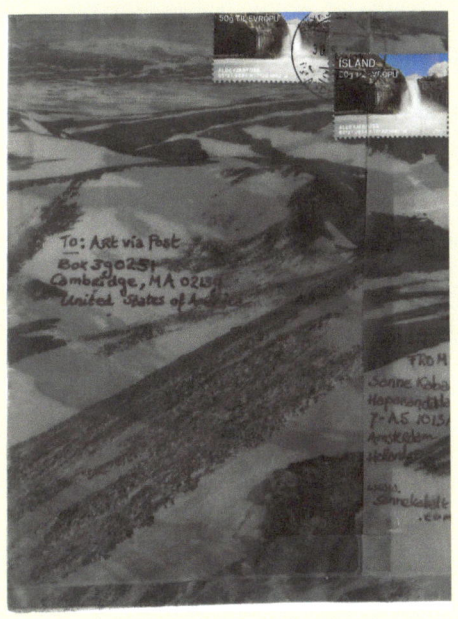
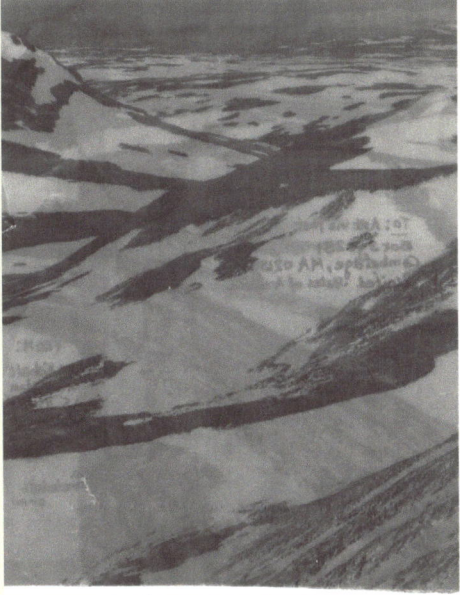

REYES, FANNY KATHY

Chicago, Illinois

KABALT, SANNE

Amserdam, Holland

sanrekabalt.com

BUCHHOLZ, JOACHIM

Berlin, Germany

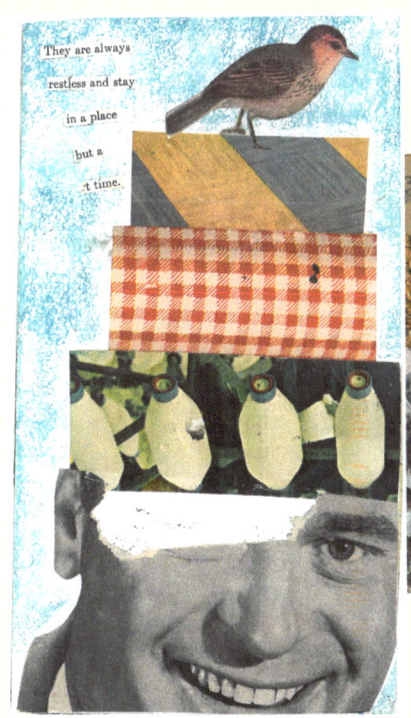

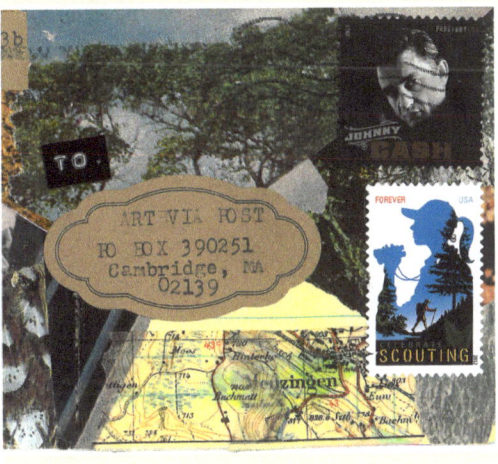

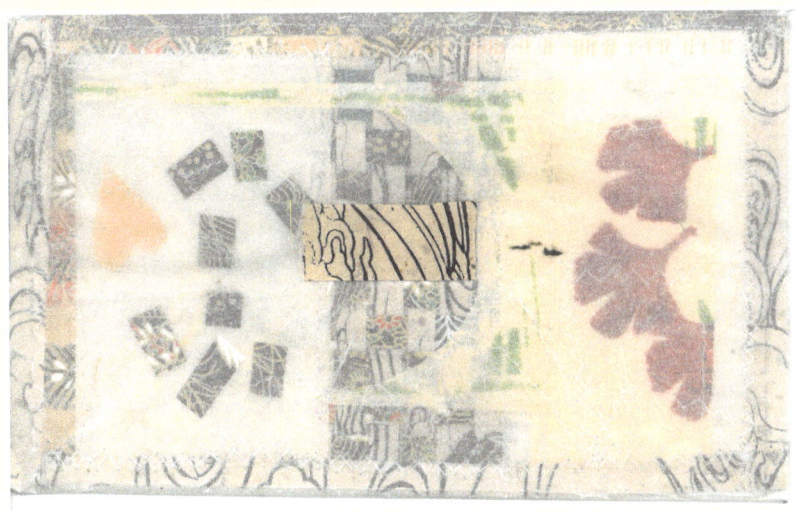

OLSON

Brooklyn, New York

CHURCHILL, NICCELA

Alberta, Canada

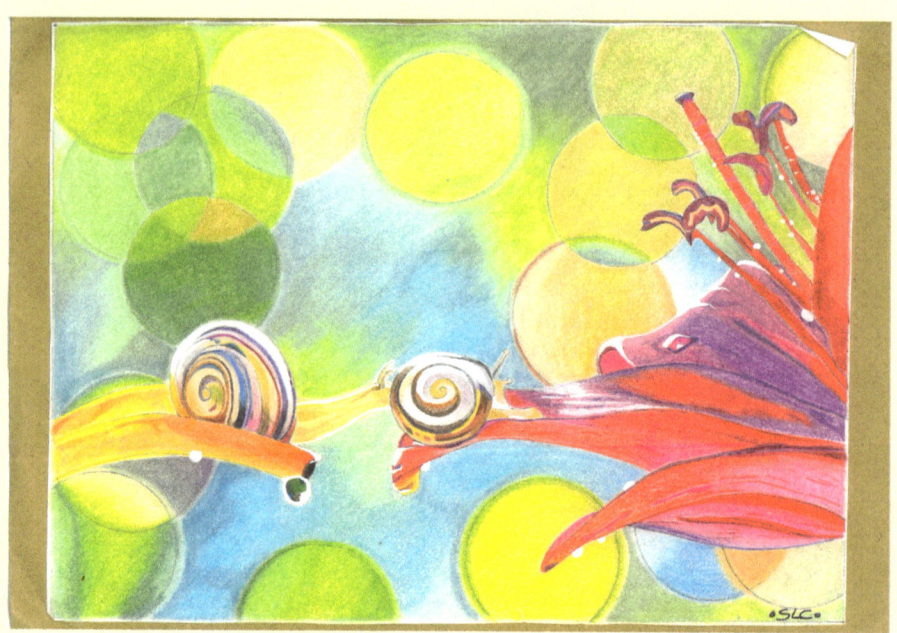

"I think mail art is the most fun way to spread love for art. Can you image how many people hand a piece of mail art? My submission wanted to show the love and support we should have one to each other. If even a tiny snail can push and support another, what does it make impossible to us?" - Sara Carbonara

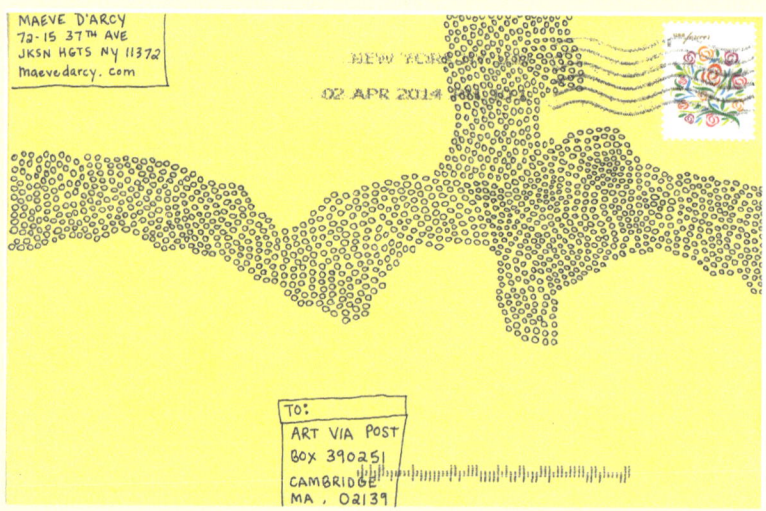

CARBONARA, SARA

Glasgow, United Kingdom

D'ARCHY, MAEVE

Jackson Heights, New York

maevedarcy.com

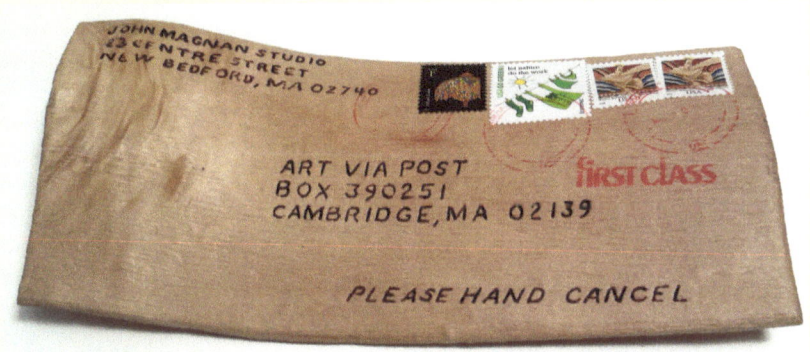

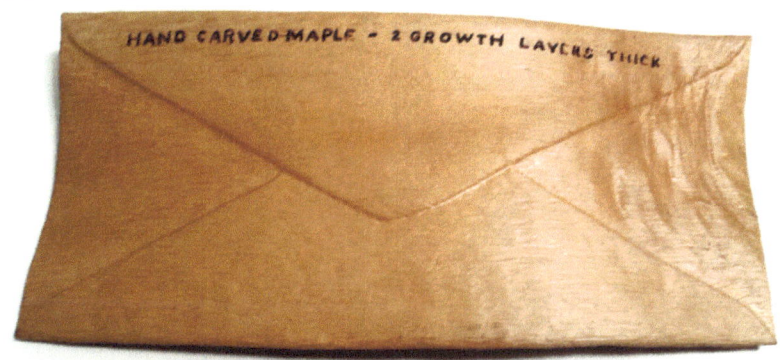

"Art via Post offered an opportunity to create and share work having multiple layers of concept. As I wood sculptor, I knew immediately that I would submit a wooden envelope, but found myself considering the question of what makes something a letter, and where is the content located? The idea deepened when I decided to carve it following the growth rings of the tree from which the wood came. The sculpture is two growth layers thick, detailed to look like an envelope. My "letter" cannot be opened, but the layers themselves are content, bearing witness to two years in the life of a maple tree that once lived. All the curves and ripples are memories of the tree as it grew. And of course, our familiar envelopes are made of paper, which comes from trees, so we seem to have come full circle. Mailing the letter, seeing it hand stamped and sent off into the USPS further validated its status. Nonetheless, where is the content? What is a letter? I still am not sure." -John Magnan

MAGNAN, JOHN

New Bedford, Massachusetts

johnmagnan.com

facebook: john magnan studio

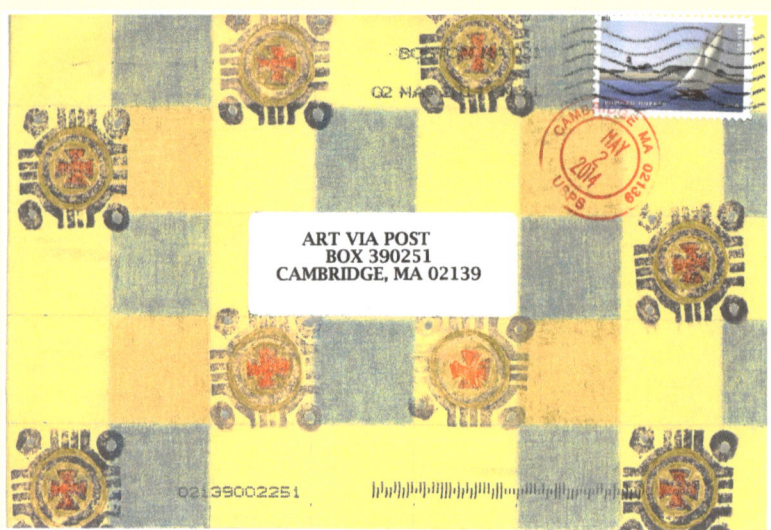

"I am a painter and have always been drawn to the paraphernalia surrounding snail mail, i.e. envelopes, postage, drawing and writing tools. Coincidentally, my father was a stamp collector. Over the years I've done collages incorporating his stamps and other ephemera. ArtviaPost's call to artists definitely appealed to me." - Toby Atlas

ATLAS, TOBY

Cambridge, MA

tobyatlas.com

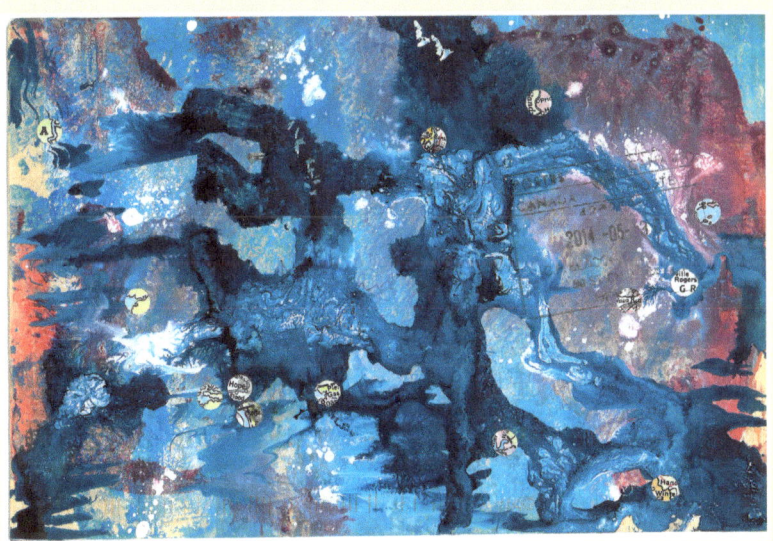

"I am a mixed media artist also involved in the book arts. However, it is as an armchair traveller that mail art offers the opportunity to satisfy my curiosity about other places and people. The theme, "Envelope as Art", piqued my interest and generated questions as to the nature of the container and contents. If the envelope holds all the needed information and artwork, what do you put on the inside?" - Marina Bancroft

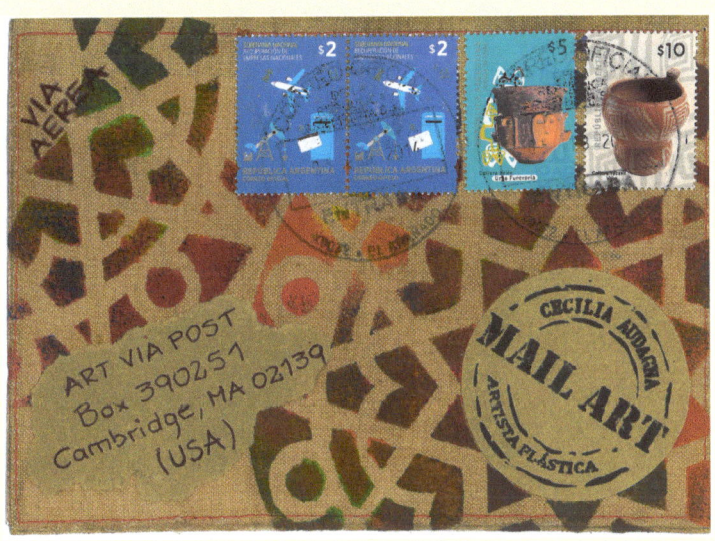

BANCROFT, MARINA

Quebec, Canada

marinabancroft.com

AUDAGNA, CECILIA

Argentina

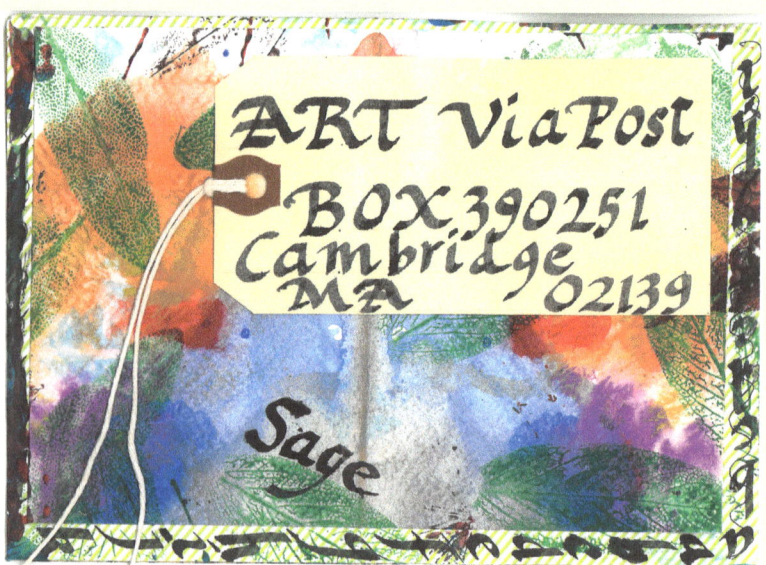

NORTHROP, JOY HOLDER

Michigan

autumnsensation.etsy.com

VIIZCARRA, SUSANA

Madison, Alabama

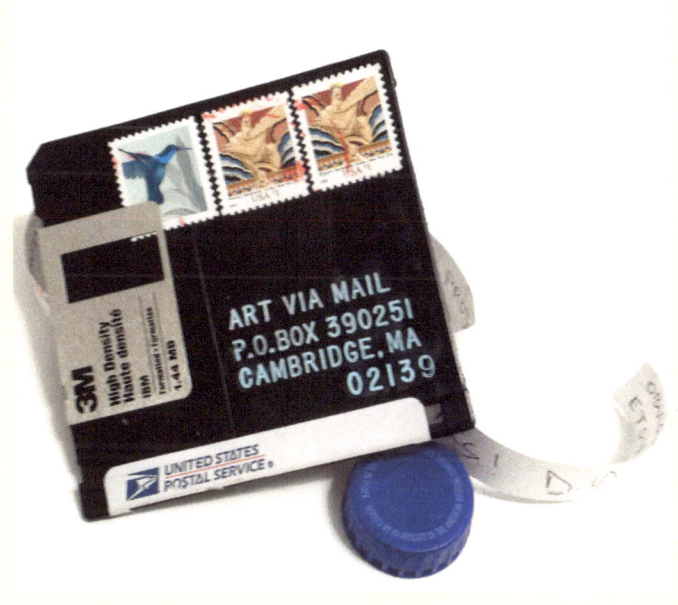

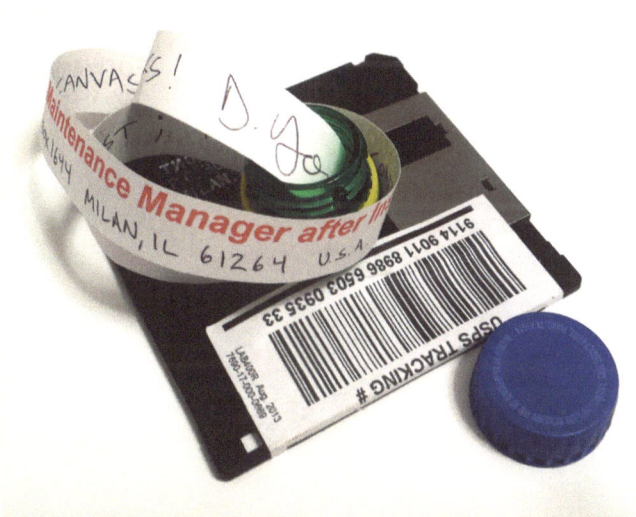

OBVIOUS FRONT

Milan, Illinois

obviousfront.com

facebook: obvious-front

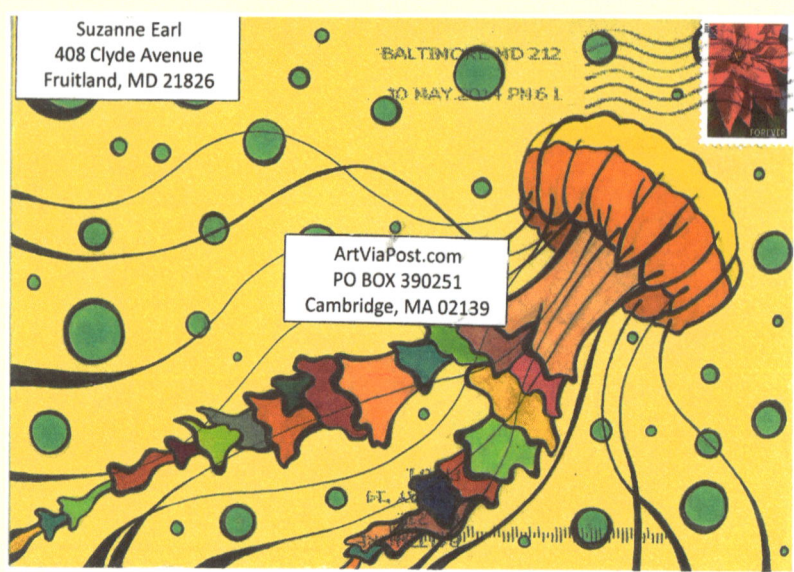

Suzanne Earl
408 Clyde Avenue
Fruitland, MD 21826

ArtViaPost.com
PO BOX 390251
Cambridge, MA 02139

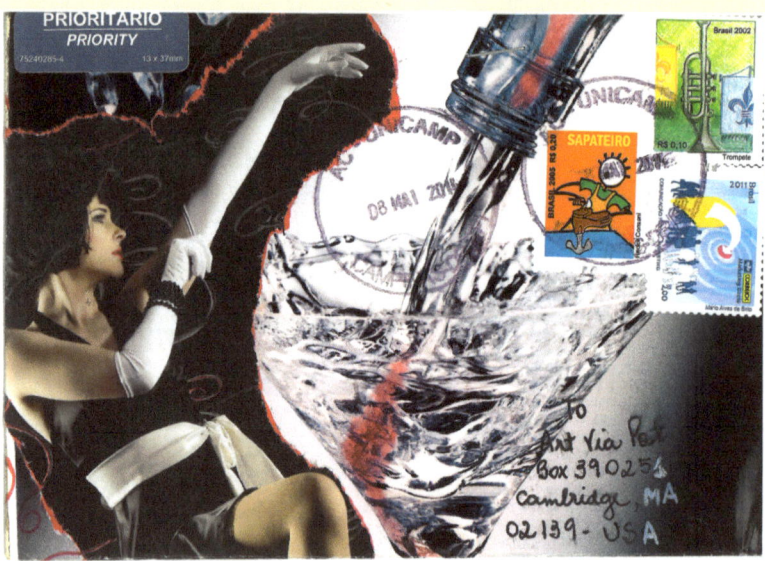

EARL, SUZANNE

Baltimore, Maryland

suzanneearl.com

GOMEZ, L.

Brazil

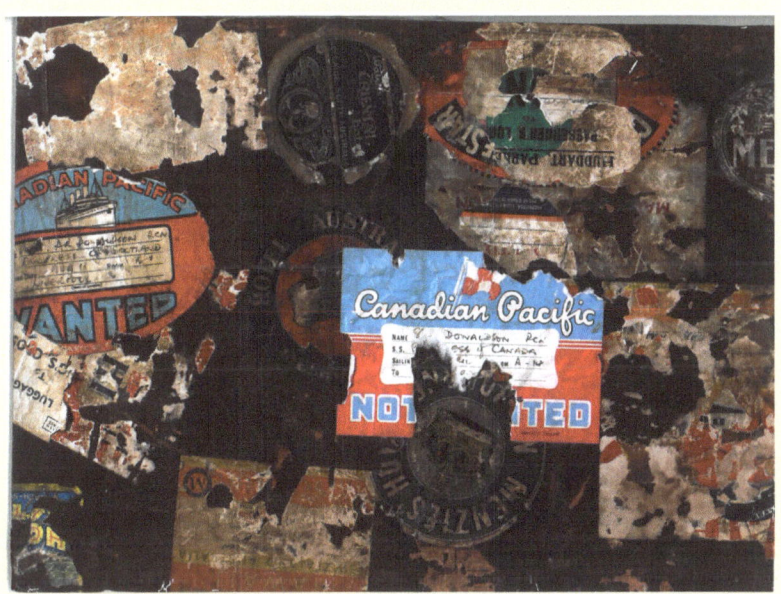

"It was my first time doing mail art and loved the concept since we help art travelling throught the world. I followed my habits about inspiration and techniques which are represented by pure colors and love for music and travels. That man travelled on his horse from Québec to Cambridge, Massachusetts to express my passion for arts." - Genevieve Garnand

---

ROUVIEVE

Chicago, Illinois

GARAND, GENEVIEVE

Canada

Facebook: genegarand

genegarand.com

"I started my mail art journey in early 2013. I have been involved in art all of my life, and after some major life events decided life is about as good as you make it. Mail art is just one way to make happy ripples in the pond of life. Please don't think this as a trite statement - live long enough, and you too, will reduce daily life to a simple motivation, "Happy ripples," is mine. I thoroughly enjoy trading art through the mails with many artists throughout the world, and will very likely continue to do so as long as can make marks on paper; it's an activity that gives me great joy.
                        - J.M.M. Barkovich

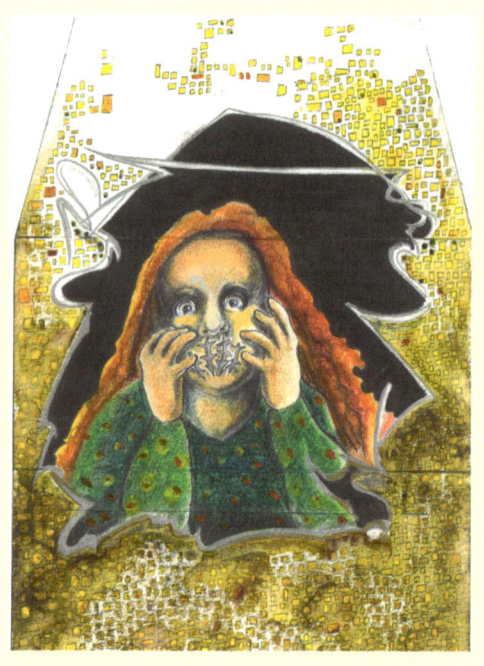

BARKOVICH, J.M.M.

Houston, Texas

jmmbarkovich.wix.com/atcs

24

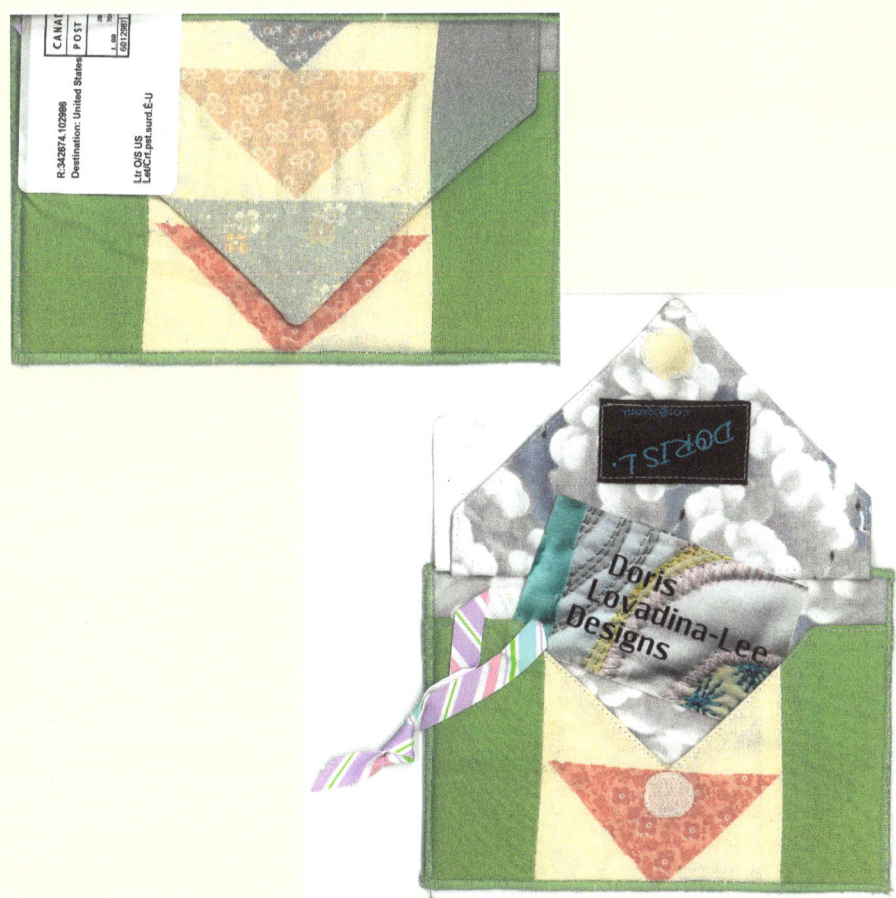

"I am a quilter that has been creating quilted postcards. These are 4" x 6" postcards, which can be sent through the mail, made using traditional quilt techniques. Each postcard is a miniature work of art, incorporating piecing, fusing, quilting, and beading. I was inspired to submit to Art via Post to challenge myself to create a postcard that incorporated the form of an envelope. My piece is made with fabric printed with a traditional quilt block: Flying Geese. I like the idea of the postcard "flying" through the postal service, arriving safely at its destination. By combining a postcard were the art and message are visible to everyone, with an envelope, the sender has the opportunity to enclose a private message to be discovered by the recipient." - Doris Lovadina-Lee

---

LOVADINA-LEE, DORIS

Canada

dorislovadianalee.com

blog.dorislovadinalee.com

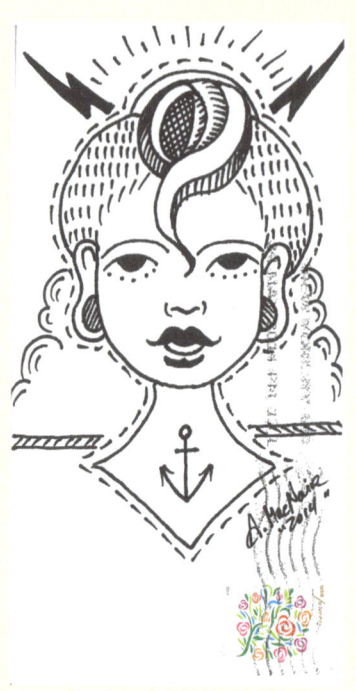

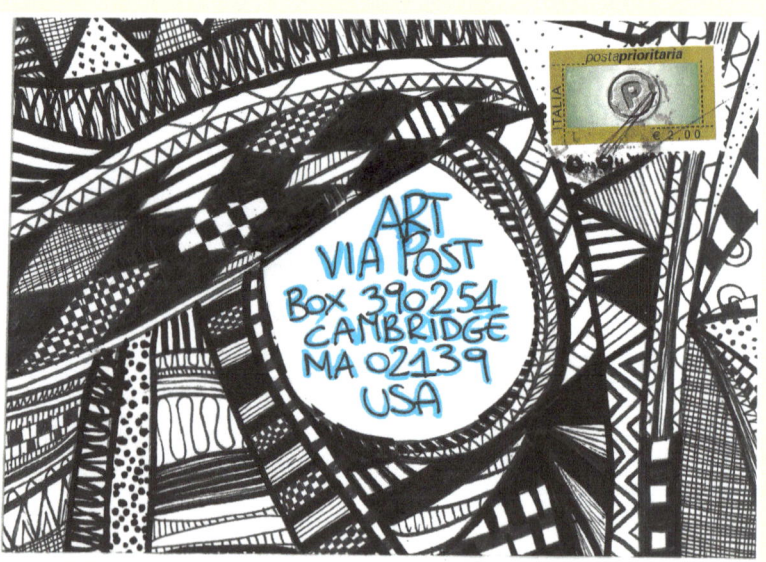

MACNAIR, A

United States

RIGHINI, TEA

Italy

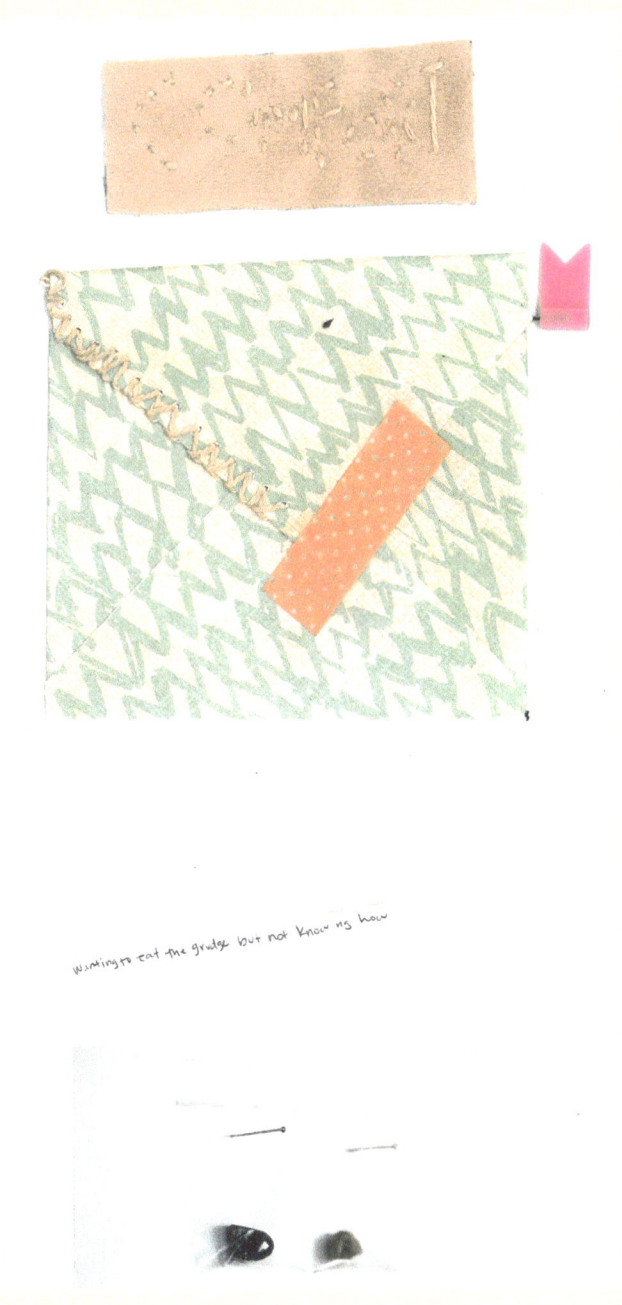

wanting to eat the grudge but not knowing how

FOWLER, TRACI

Chicago, Ilinois

tracifowler.birb.com

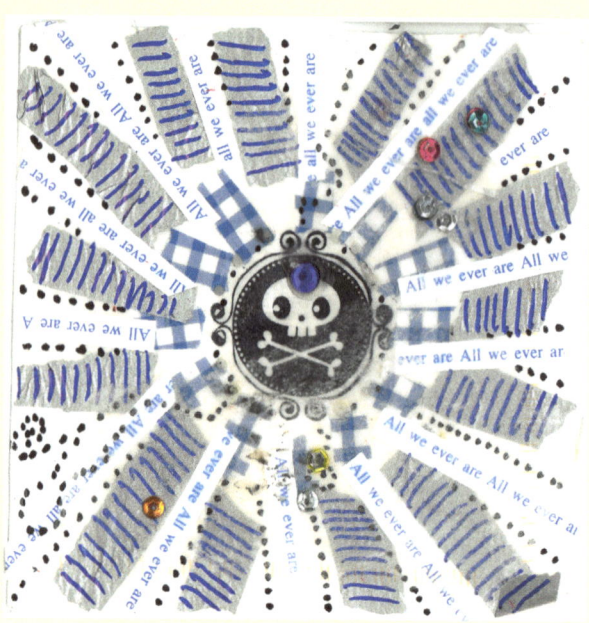

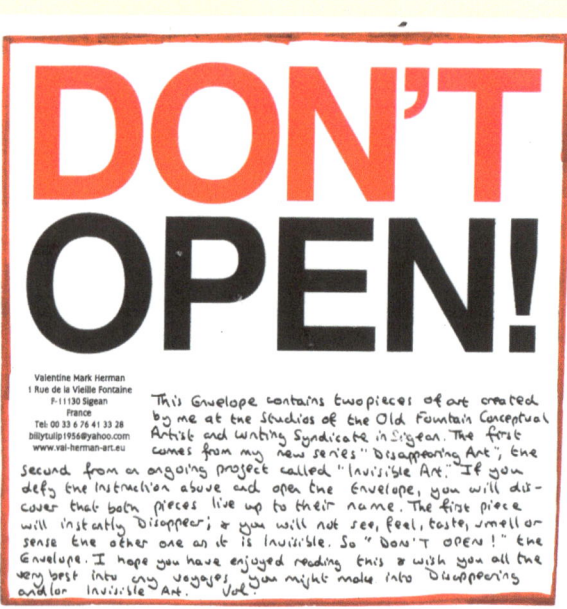

SOUP, JENNY

San luis, California

HERMAN, VALENTINE

France

val-herman-art.eu

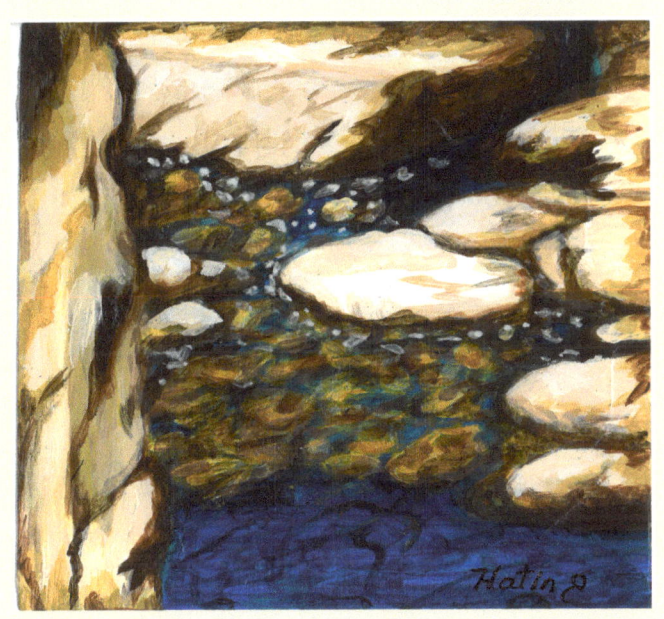

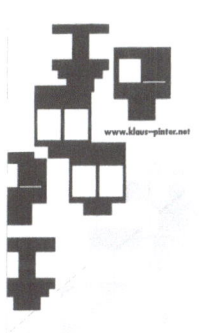
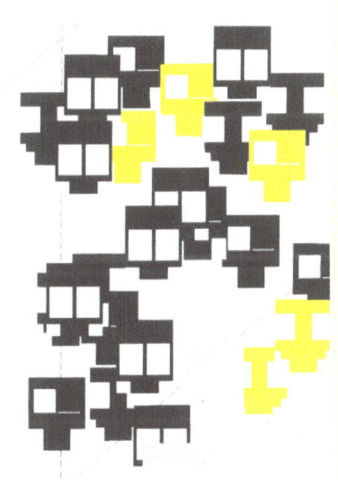

DATIN, JASIE

Canada

larthatinjosee.blogspot.ca

PINTER, KLAUS

Austria

klaus-pinter.net

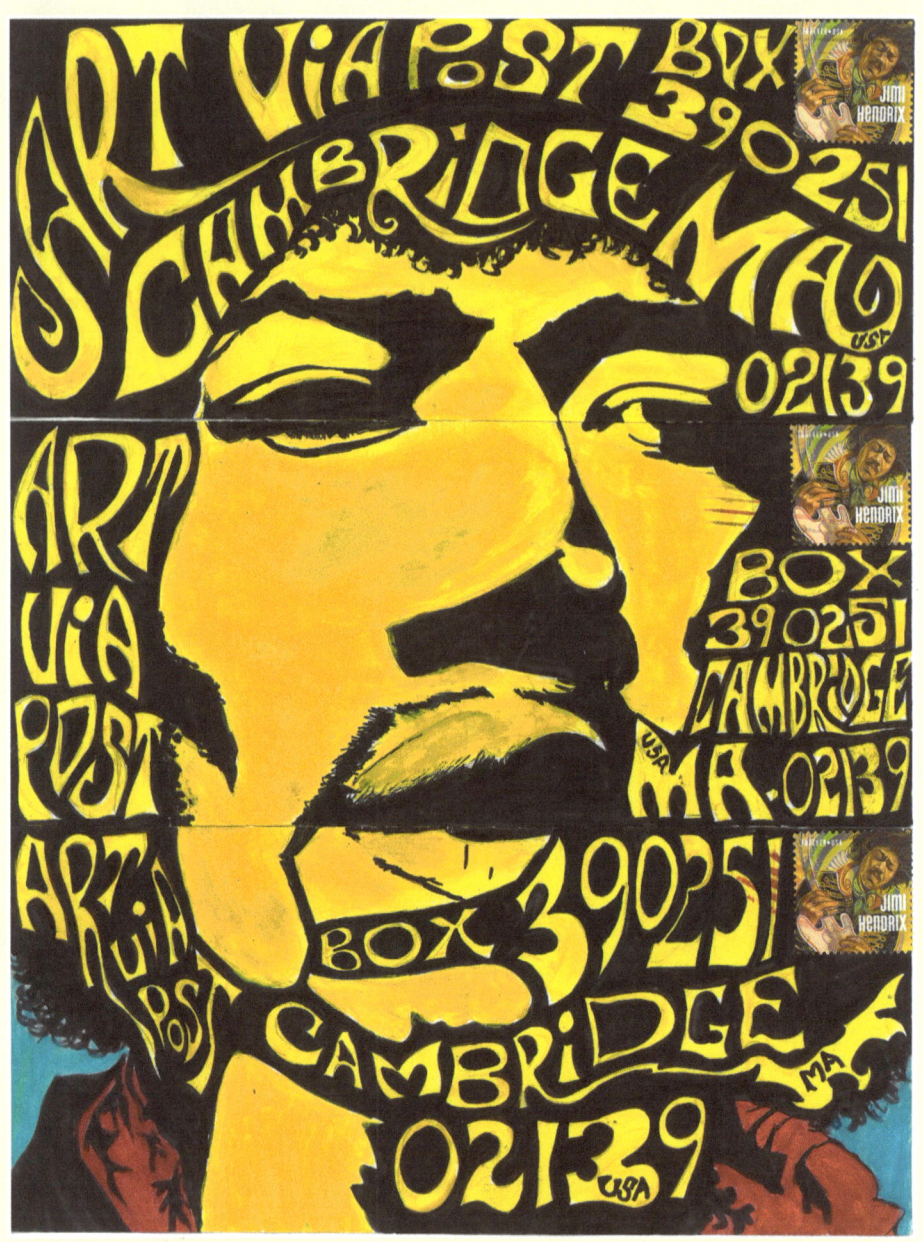

NYAGA, CAROLINE

Brighton, Massachusetts

eliyagraphics.weebly.com

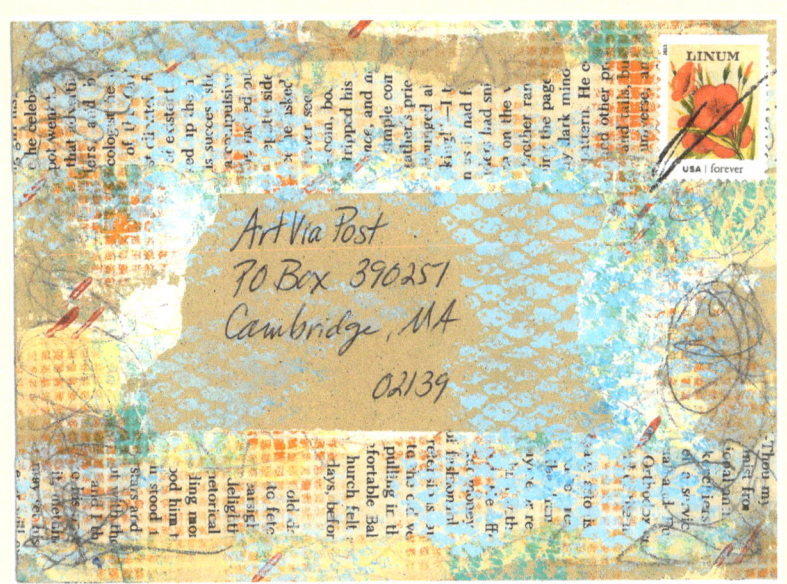

Art Via Post
PO Box 390251
Cambridge, MA

02139

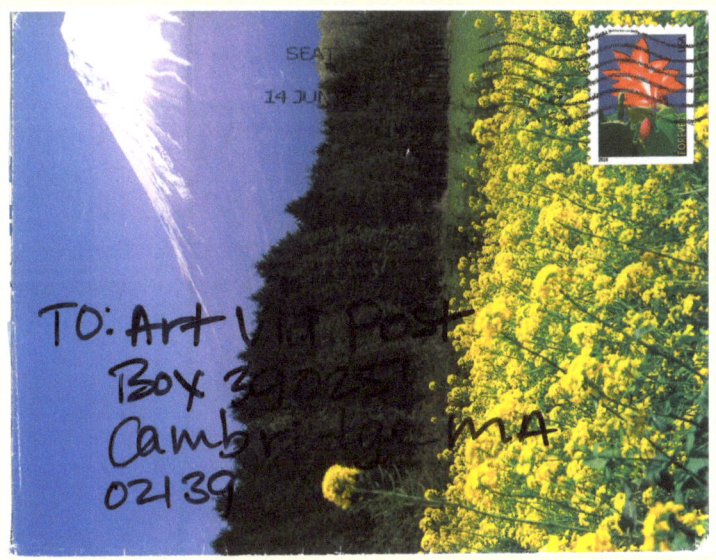

TO: Art Via Post
Box 390251
Cambridge MA
02139

BROWN, REBECCA K.

New Hampshire

EAT THE FINE PRINT

Seattle, Washington

Instagram: @eatthefineprint

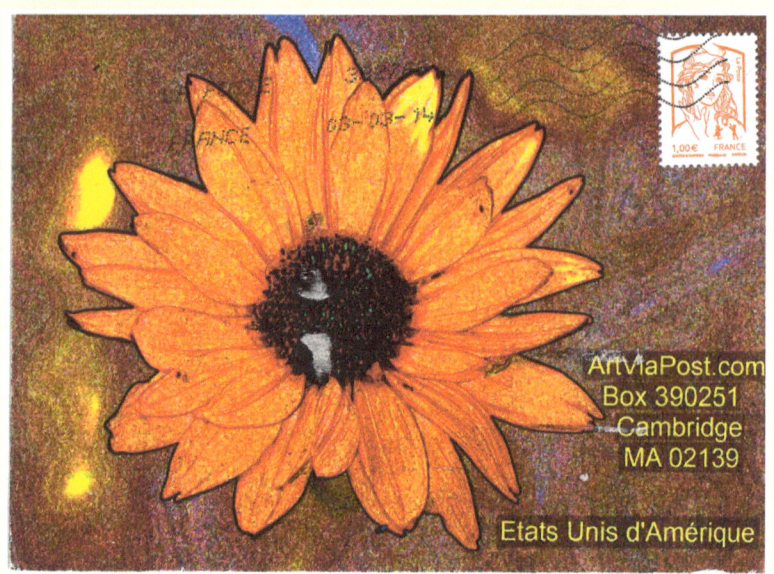

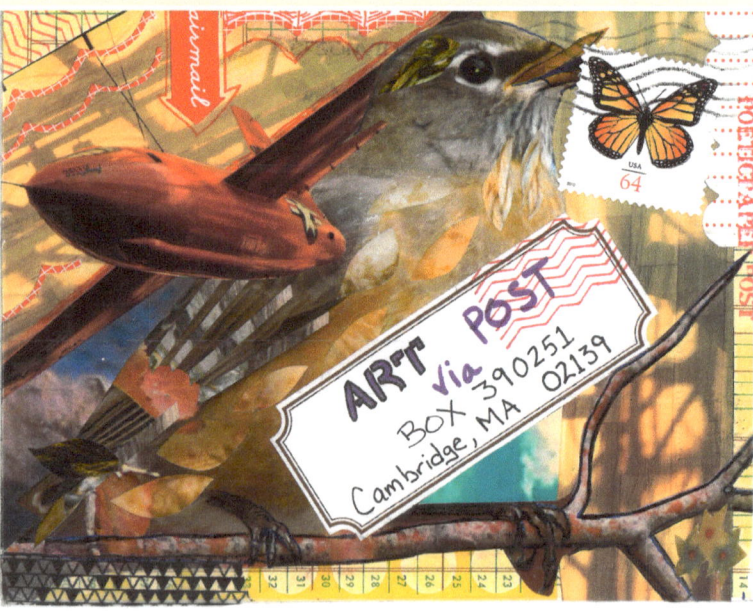

BRUTH, ERIC

France

LEE, BETHANY

Fleming Island, Florida

poeticpaperpost.blogspot.com

ILIS, ERIN

Brazil

HORN, ANDREAS

Germany

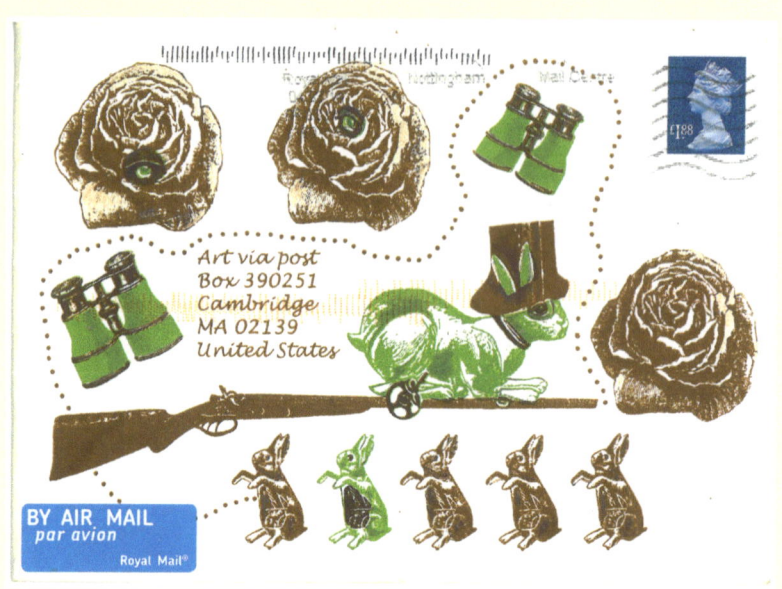

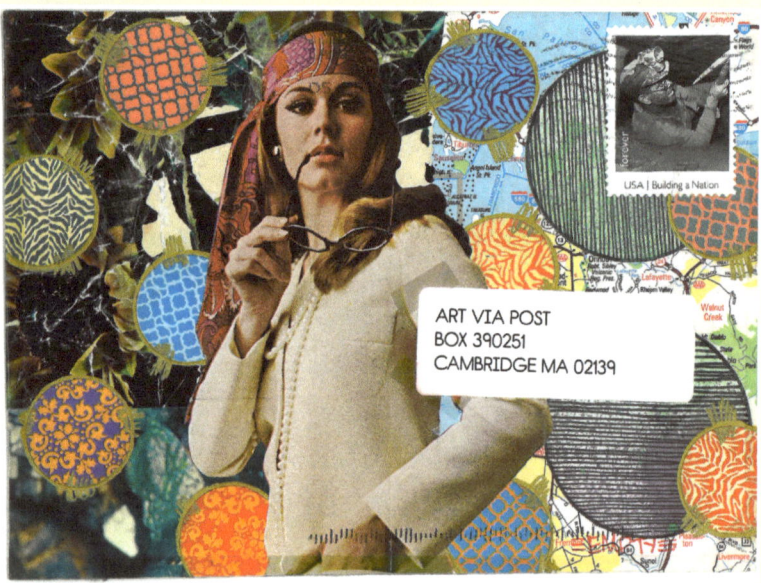

MCNANEY, NICKI

England

DODSON, STEPHANIE

Tallahassee, Florida

stephart.tumblr.com

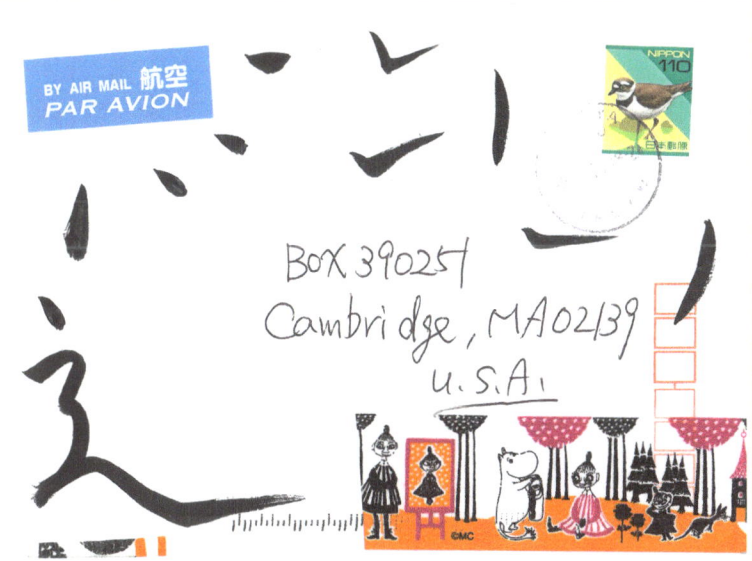

"I mail art because I am enjoying to create collaborative works with other artists. I am also enjoying to look other senses and images. I am inspired by other feelings or senses of other mail artists. Networking by Post is very exiting for me." - Keiichi Nakamura

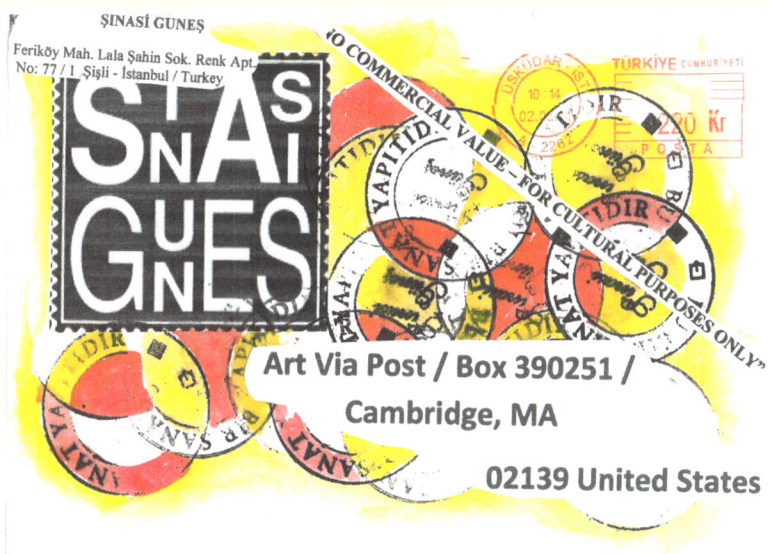

NAKAMURA, KEIICHI

Tokyo, Japan

GUNES, SINASI

Istanbul, Turkey

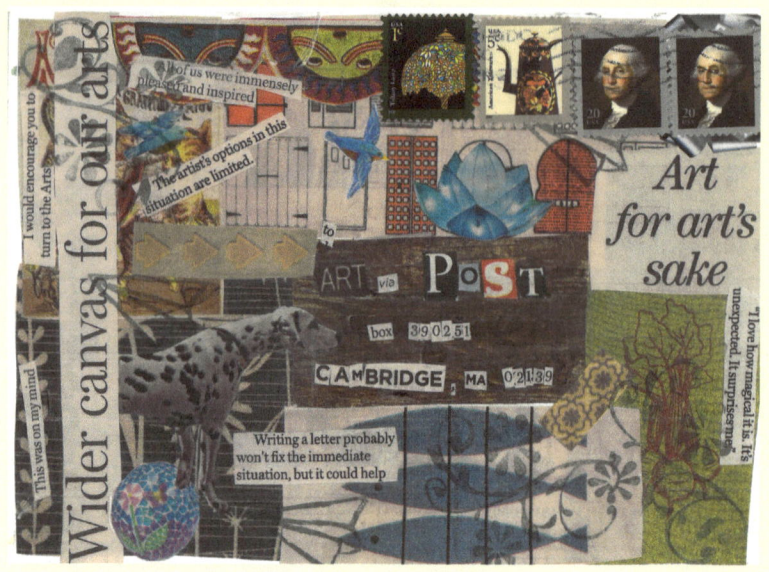

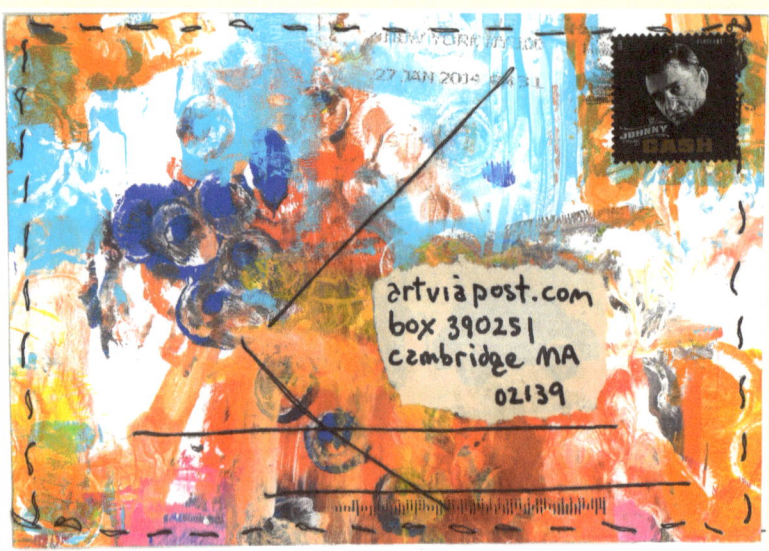

BARAK, SARAH

Dallas, Texas

Instagram: @letter_writer

WILLIAMS, MEEAH

Brooklyn, New York

walkingeyeball.blogspot.com

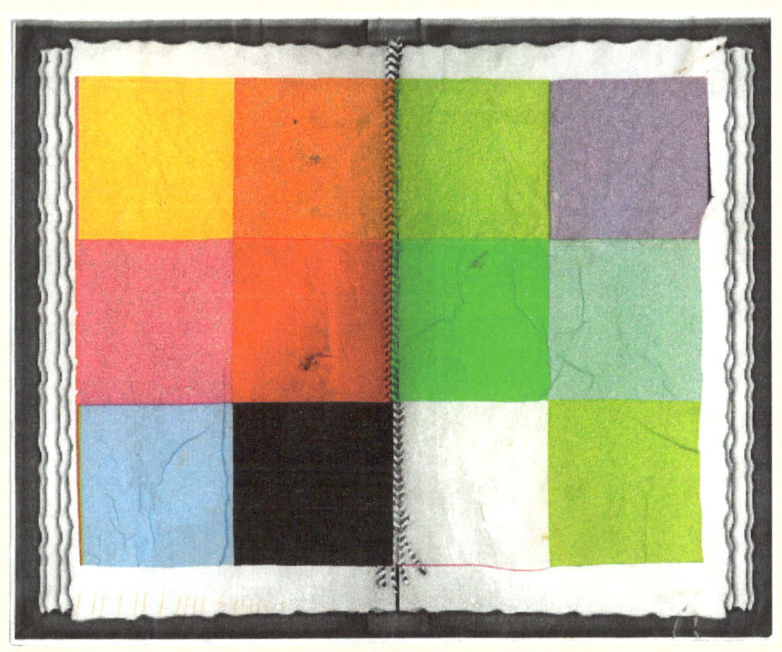

KRAUS, WOLFGANG

Munich, Germany

PERIONE, SILVANO

Genoa, Italy

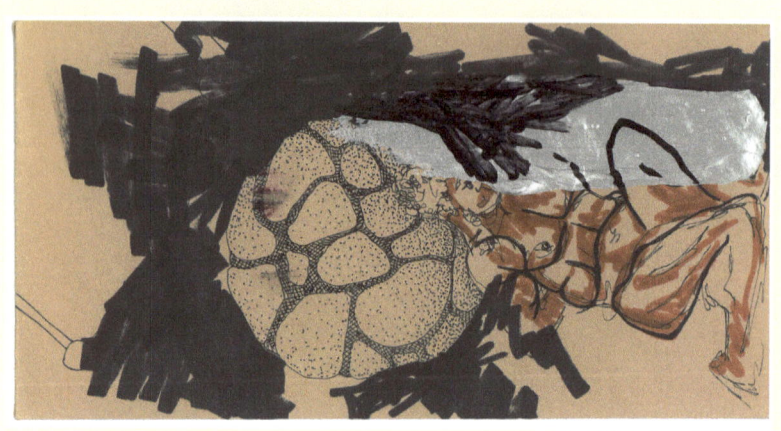

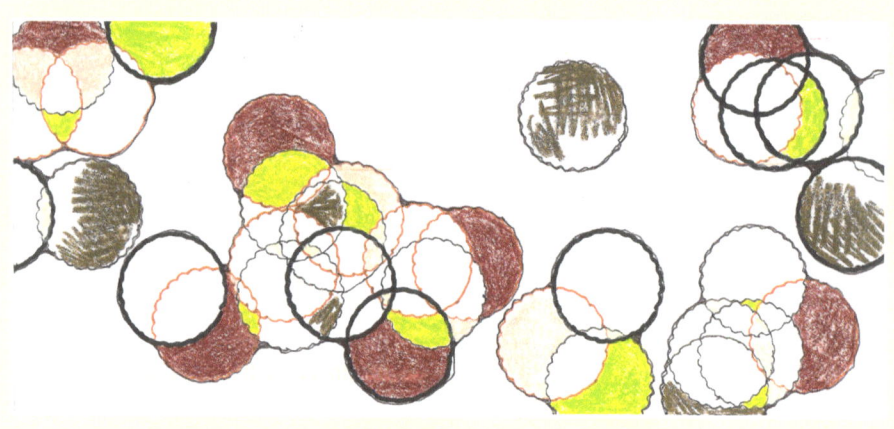

STAMM, T.

Portland, Maine

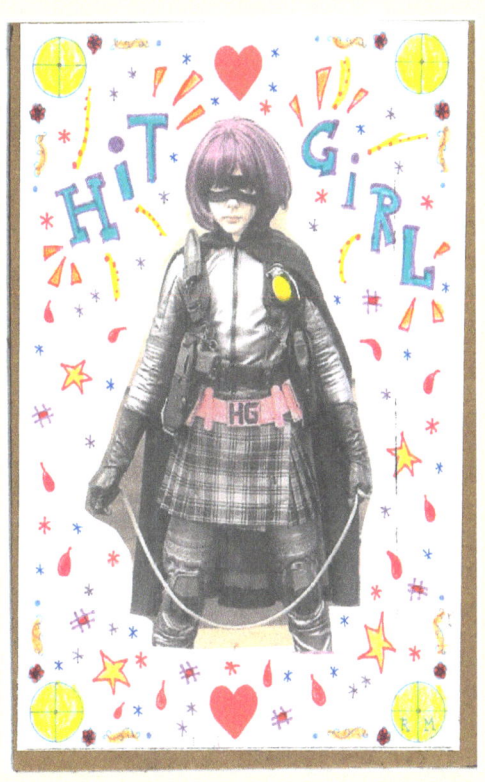

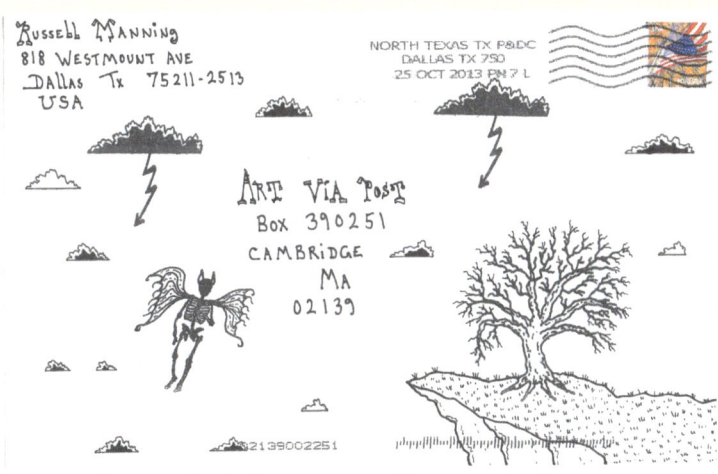

MANNING, RUSSELL

Dallas, Texas

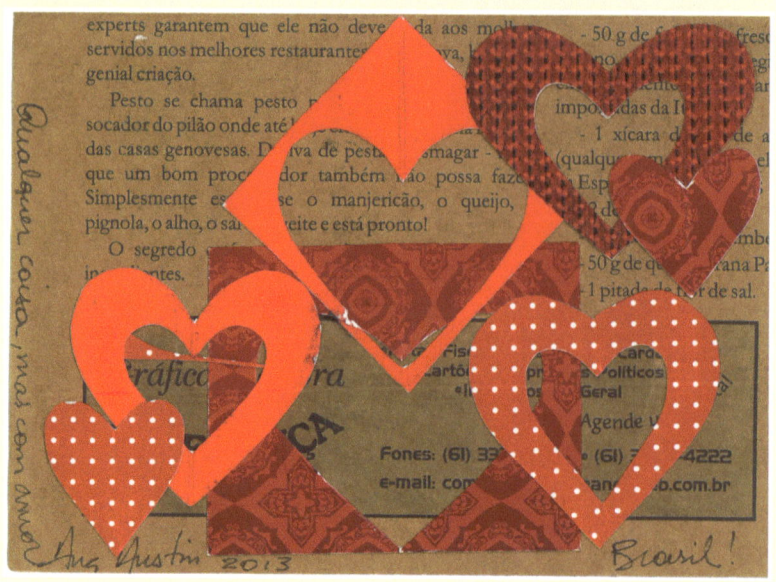

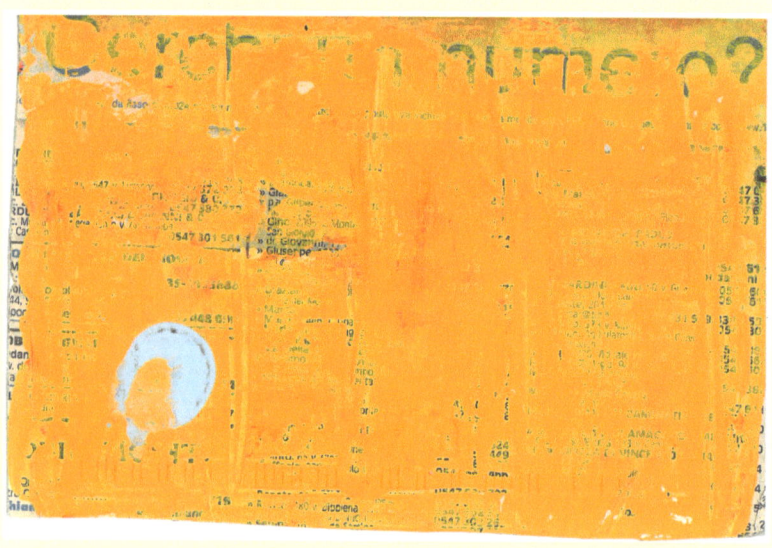

AUSTIN, ANA MARTA

Brazil

anamartaustin.blogspot.com

CONTE, ANTONIO

Naples, Italy

40

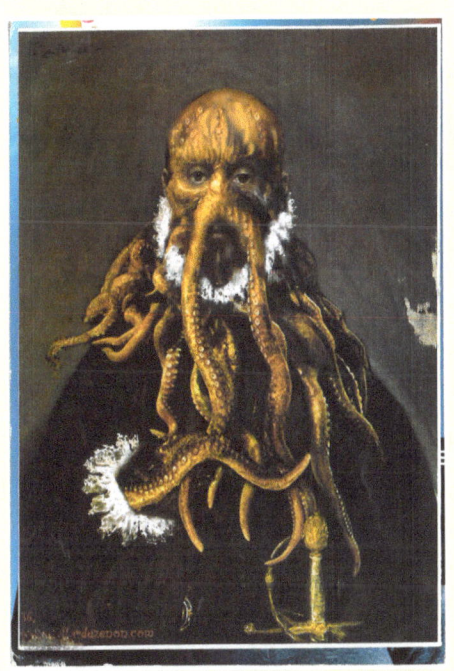

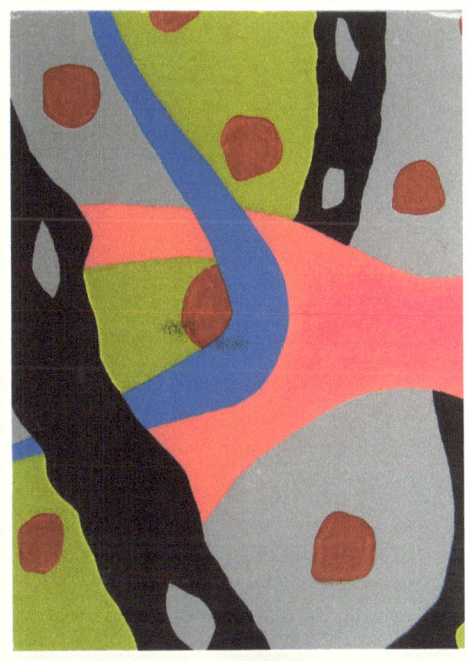

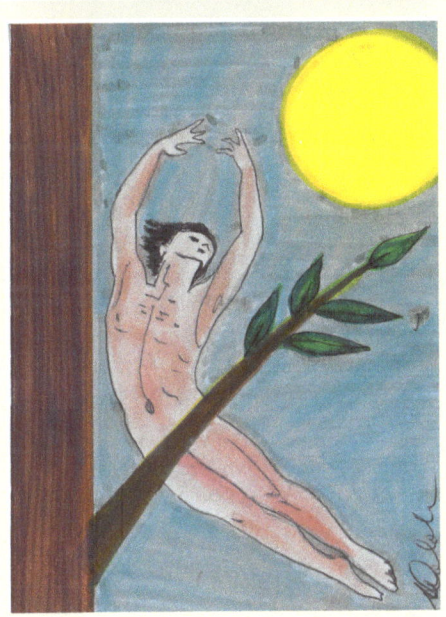

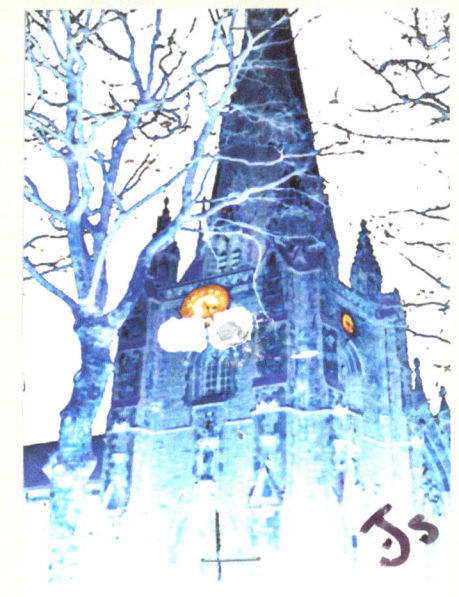

JIMENEZ, MIGUEL
Sevile, Spain
CALABRESE, ANTONIA
Italy
antoniacalbrese.wordpress.com

THEUMINCK, JAN
Belgium
SCOLARO, JANEL
Santa Ana, California
pinkypostzine.wordpress.com

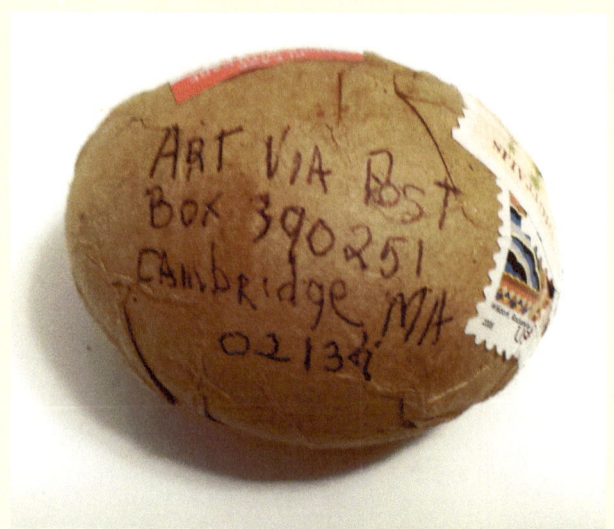

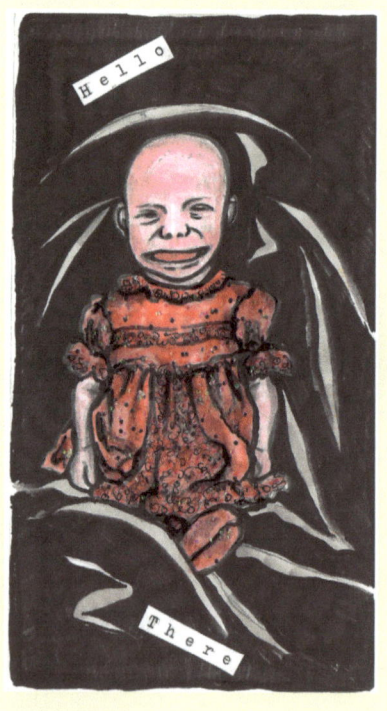

NAZZ, JAMES

New York, New York

jamesnazz.net

DENT, LILLA

Chicago, Illinois

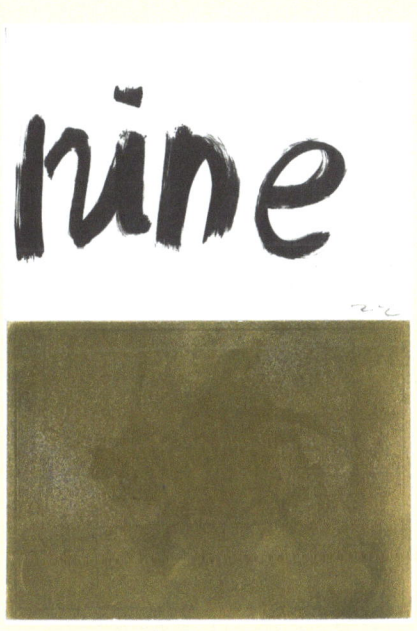

FUHRMANN, THORSTEN

Germany

art-activities.de

FALZONE, JOHANNA

New Port, Florida

johannafalzone.com

Facebook: johannafalzoneart

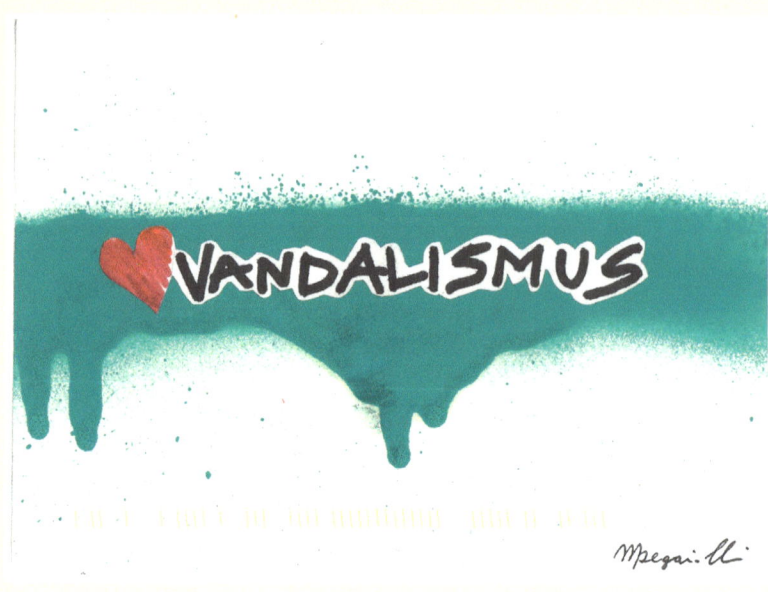

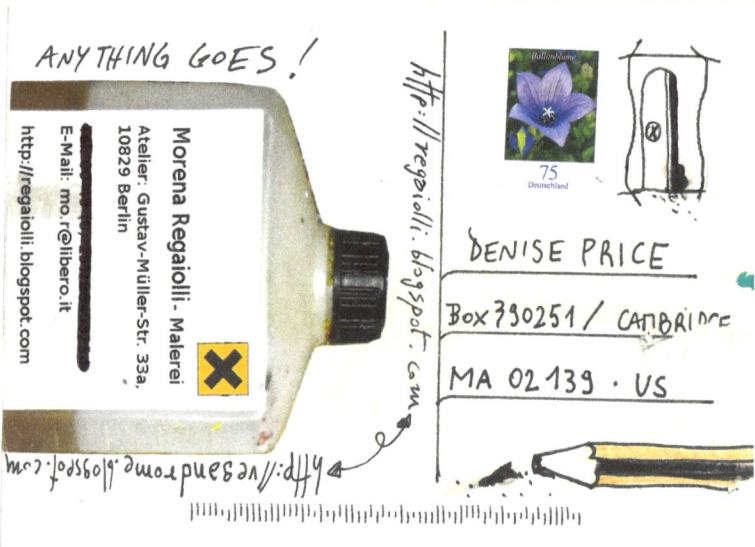

REGAIOLLI, MORENA

Berlin, Germany

Tregaiolli.blogspot.com

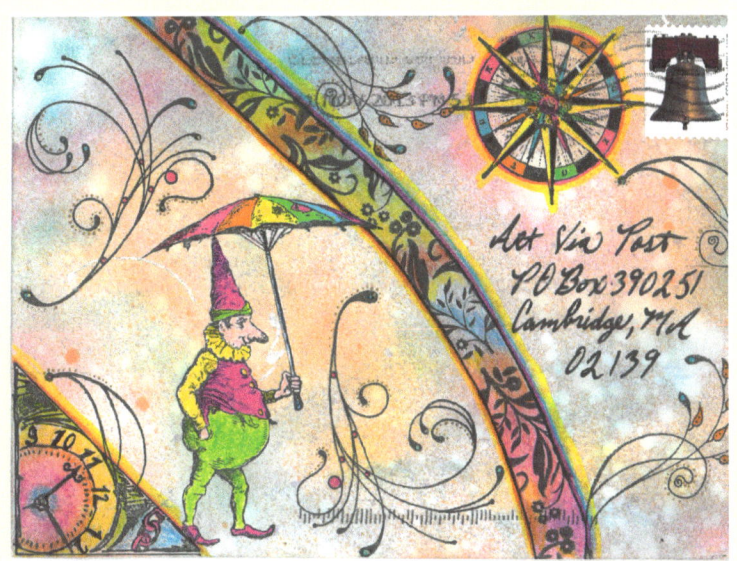

"It's plainly this: I see paper communication as a lovely, tangible thing. And what could be more romantic, surprising, engaging, amusing, distracting... than to have that special communication to arrive blatantly wrapped in ART? It expresses something that touches the recipient way more profoundly than words alone." -Mrs. Sawbones

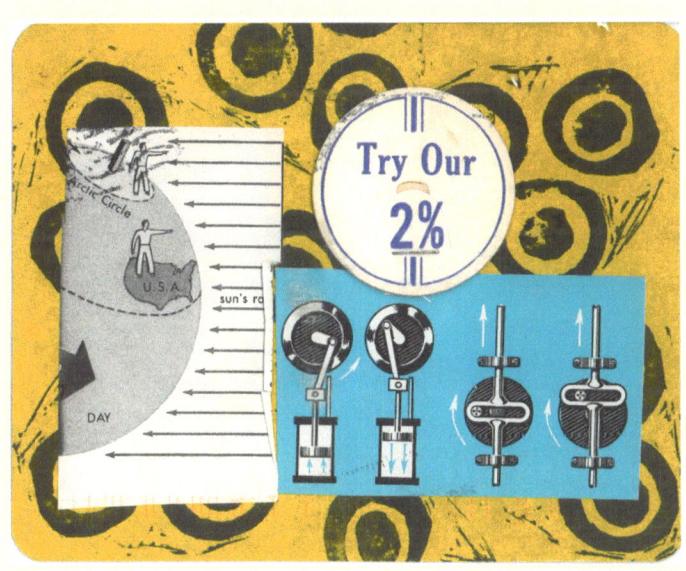

MARGARET, MARY
AKA MRS. SAWBONES

Canton, Ohio

Instagram: jellysock

MANACK, JESSICA

San Franciso, California

Instagram: jessicamanack

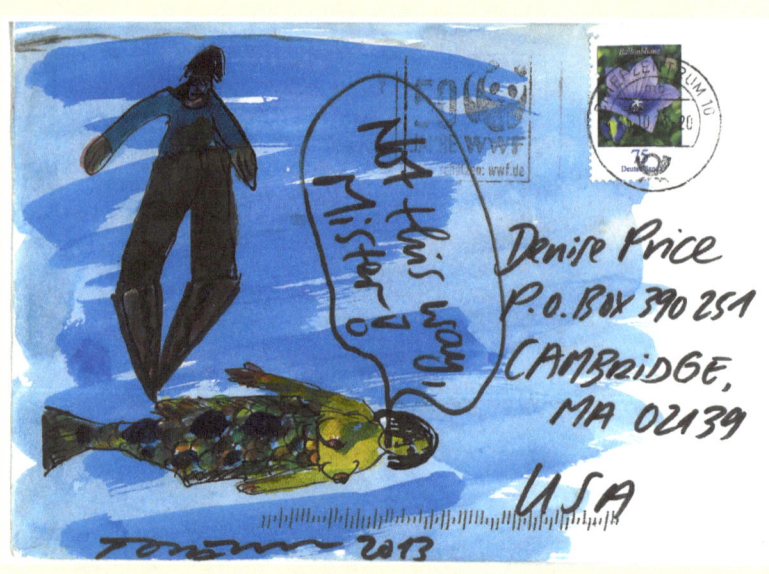

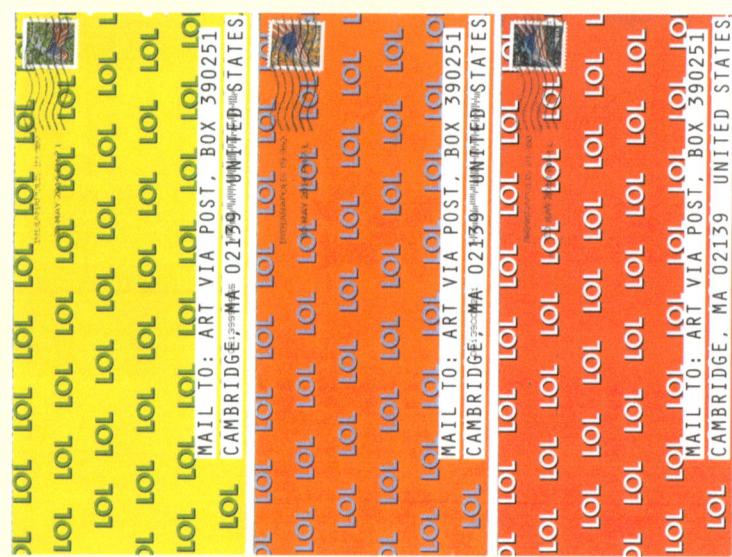

ZILLING, BERNHARD

Germany

www.bernhard-zilling.de

HERRERA, BERNADETTE

Lafayette, Indiana

behance.net/panoramiccolors

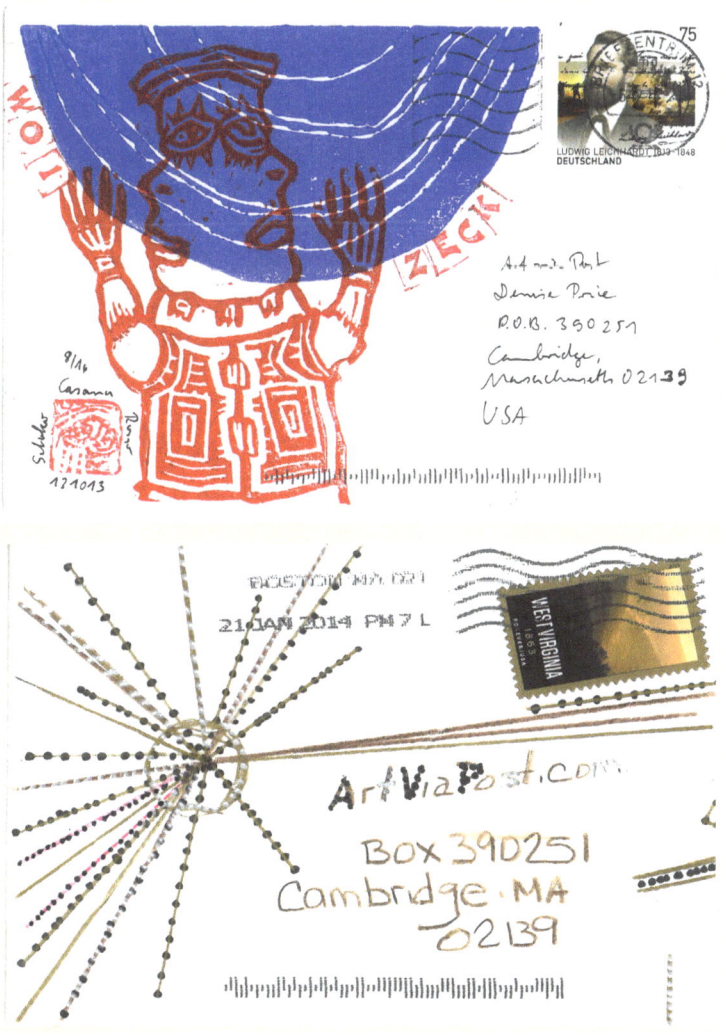

"I love to share my art and fun envelopes with people I hope will appreciate them! I love getting MAIL ART in my post office box most of all. It is always a thrill to see how other people create and share their art in the form of an envelope. Each one has such a different personality . MAIL ART can be a nice experience just taking it to the post office to get it hand stamp and seeing if the postal clerk will have a pleasant reactaction to the envelopes or if they even noitce it is not just a regular envelope." - Hester Wright

---

ROSSO, SCHOKO CASANA
Berlin, Germany

WRIGHT, HESTER
Boston, Massachusetts

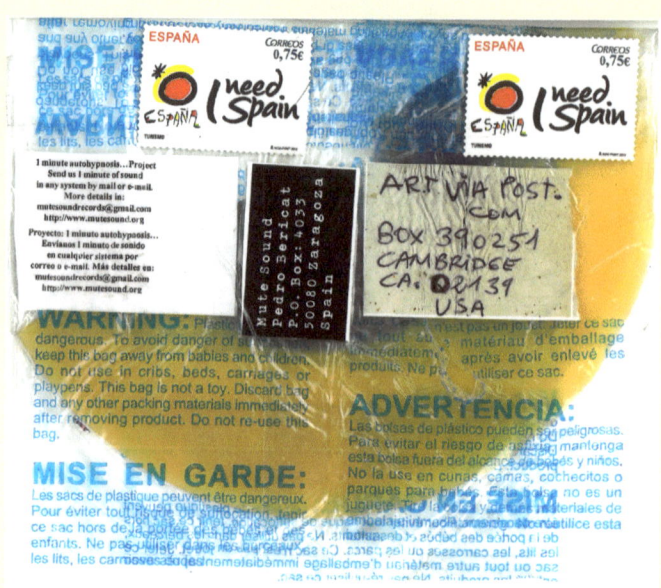

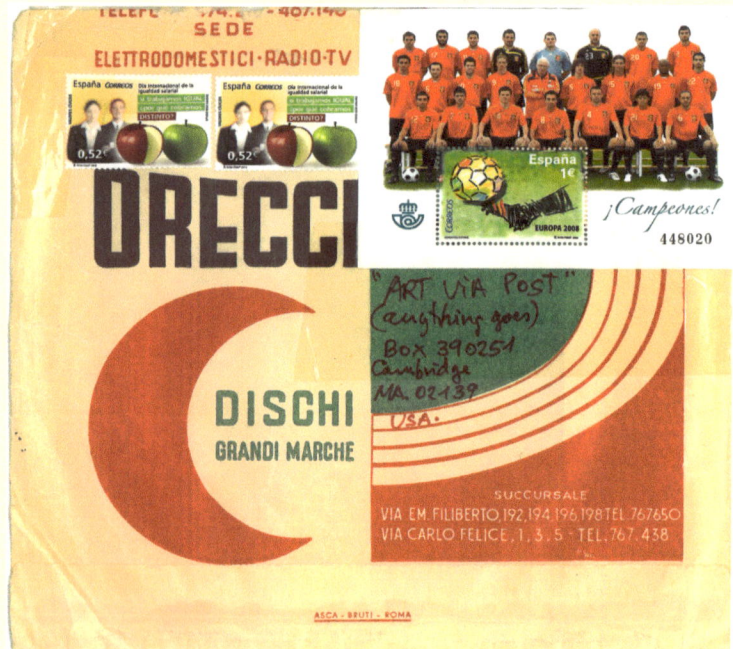

BERICAT, PEDRO

Spain

mutesound.org

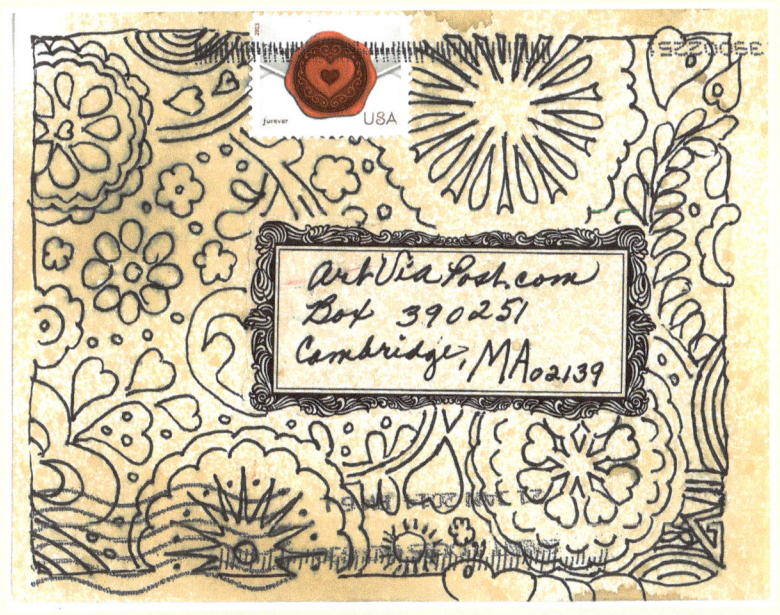

ArtViaPost.com
Box 390251
Cambridge, MA 02139

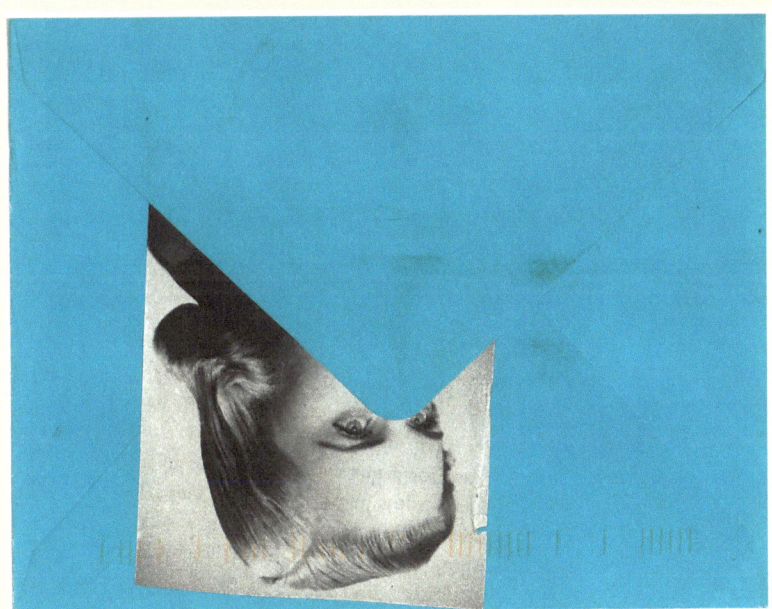

GRELLNER, MARY

Wentzville, Montana

COLLINS, LAURA

Chicago Illinois

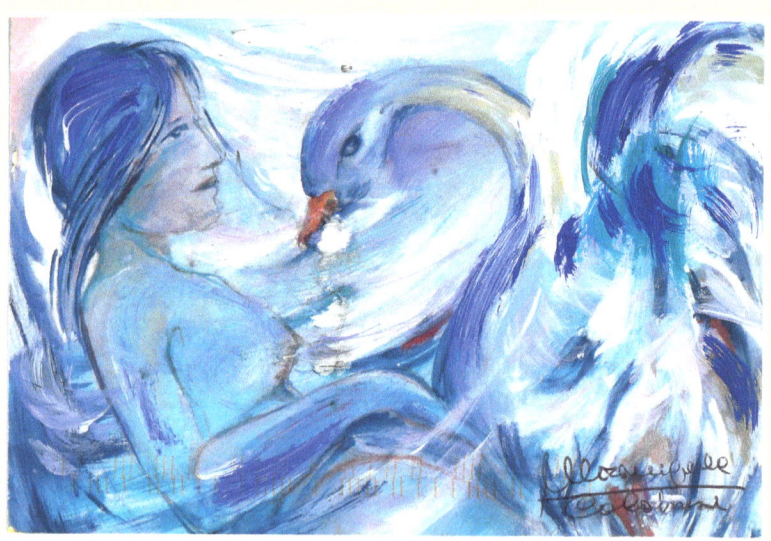

NIKOLTSOV, K.

Greece

CALABRESE, MARIANGELA

Italy

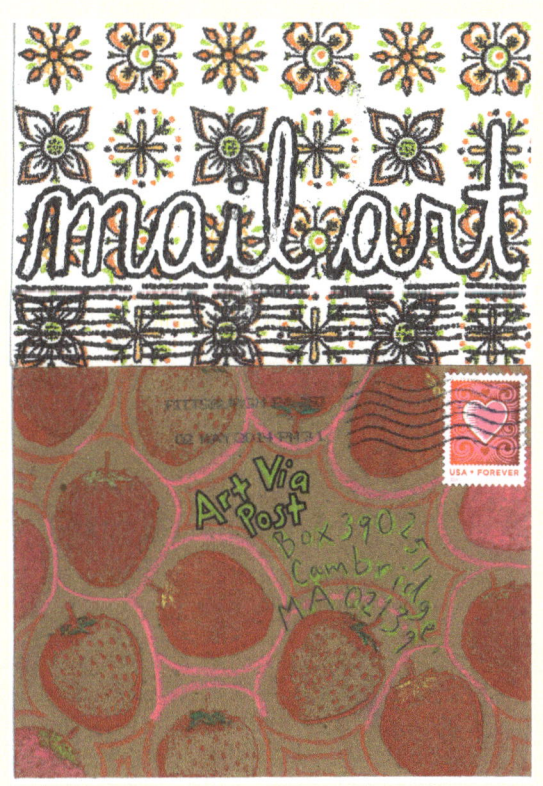

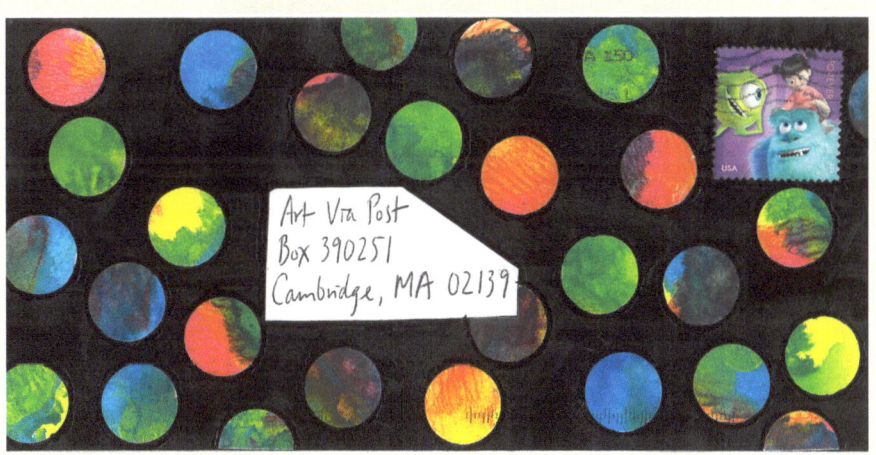

TRAN, PATTY

Pittsburg, Pennsylvania

pittsburgartistregistr.org/accounts/

view/pattytran

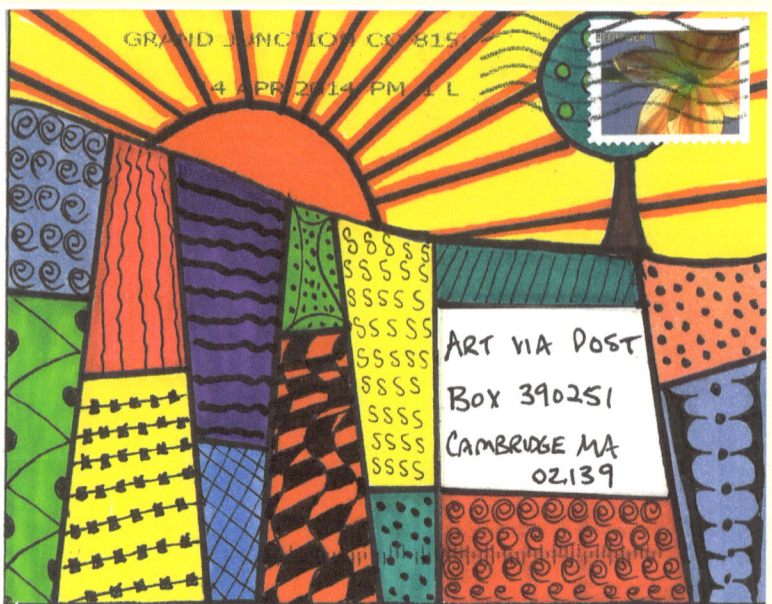

"When I create mail art, I think of all the people who will see it as it travels to its destination, and hope the serendipity of it will bring a smile to their faces. I submitted to Art via Post as a way of occupying myself while on holidays." - Terry Franks

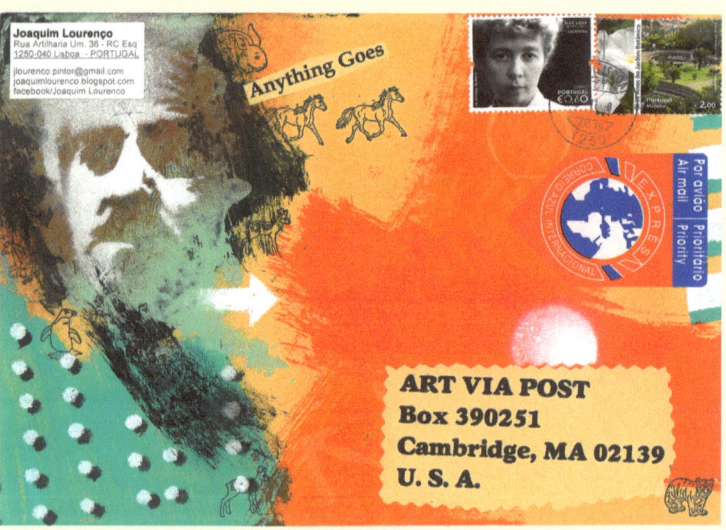

FRANKS, TERRY

Canada

LOURENCO, JOAQUIM

Portugal

Facebook: Joaquim Lourenco

joaquimlourenco.blogspot.com

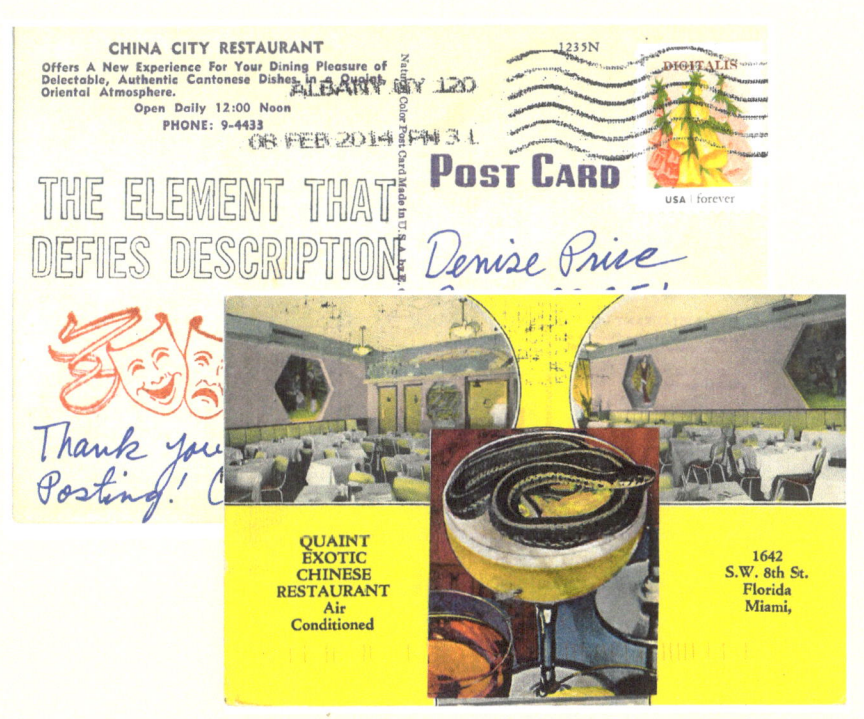

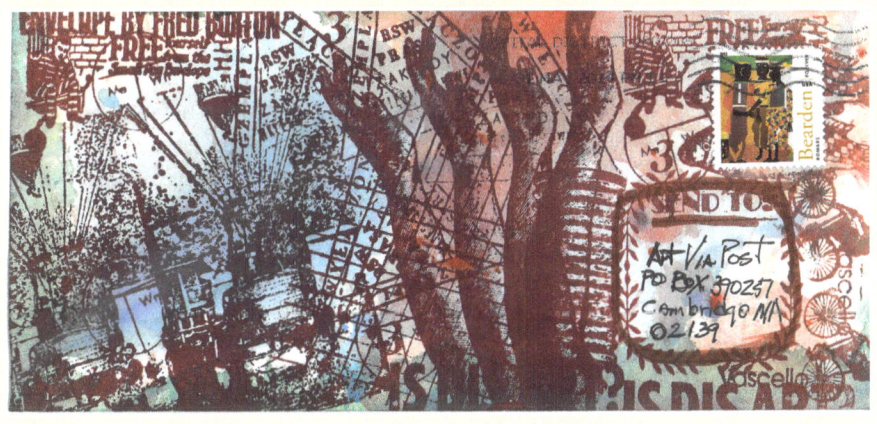

VOUTT, CAROLE

Albany, New York

BURTON, FRED

United States

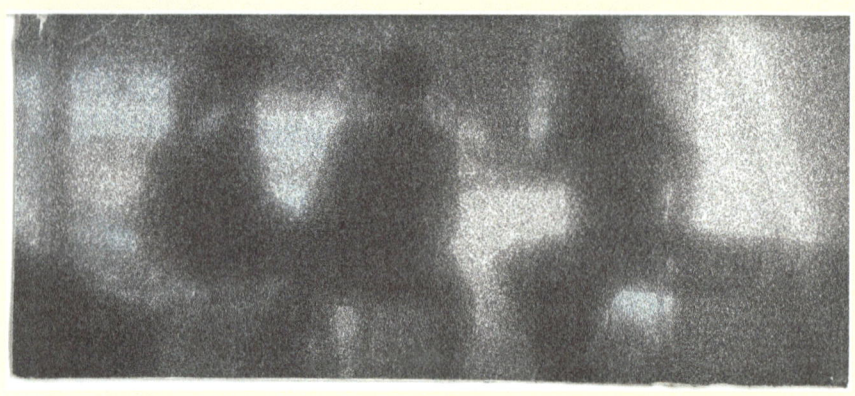

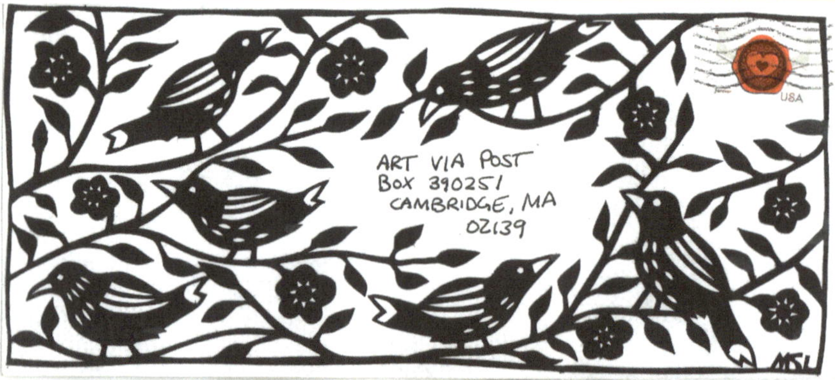

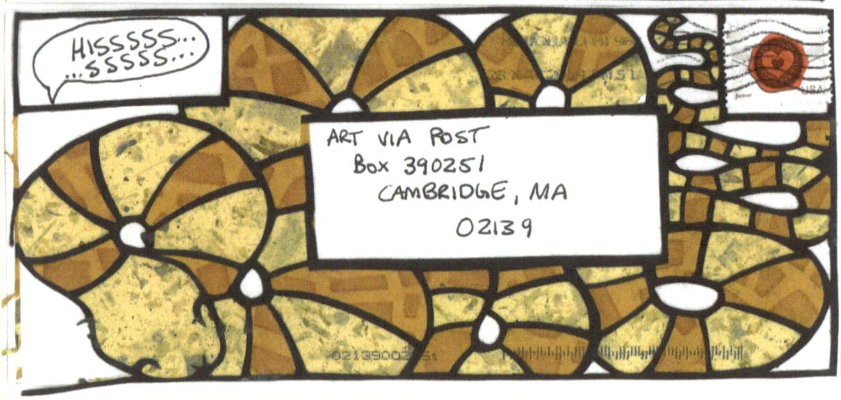

BLANKS, SLIM

Oak Park, Illinois

LOEW, MARINA

Koloa, Hawaii

falseclover.blogspot.com

facebook: False Prairie Clover

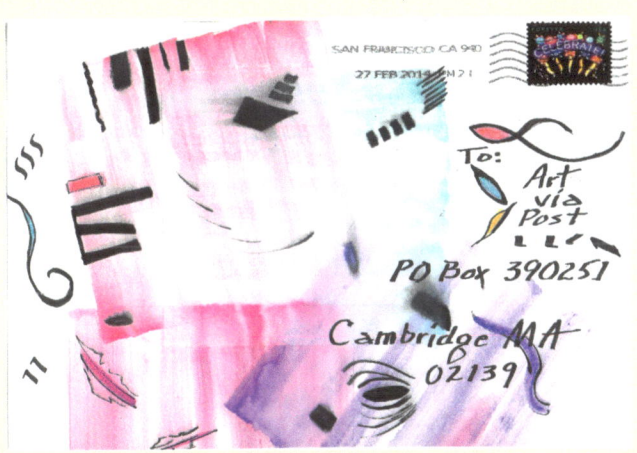

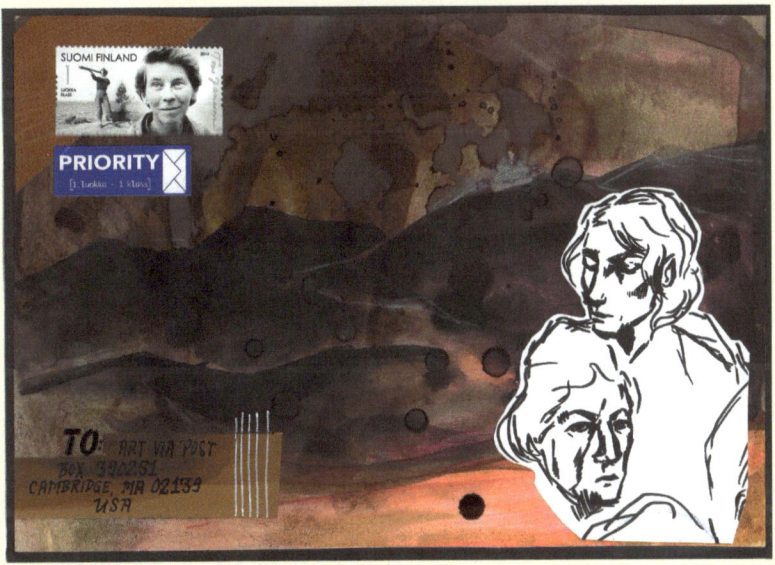

"I was introduced to the world of mail art at a young age through decos and friednship books, which are small handmade booklets that travel randomly from one artist to another, and each artist decorated a page in them. These days it's very easy to find mailart calls via Internet, so I have been frequently sending mail art envelopes and postcards for exhibitions around the world. I use mail art as my "sketchbook" of sorts, in the way that it keeps me experimenting and creating when I don't feel like painting or doing "professional" art. I'm a bookbinder and painter by trade, so the professional side of my life is closely connected with mail art."

- Elina Lundahl

RIZZULO, CARMELA

Sunnyvale, California

Decordis.art.blogspot.com

LUNDAHL, ELINA

Narva, Finland

veterok.net

ipernity.com/veterok

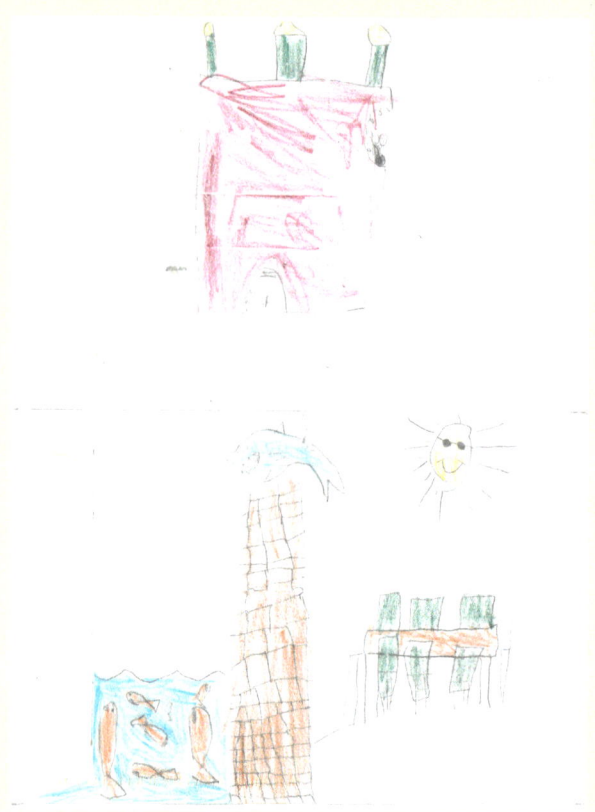

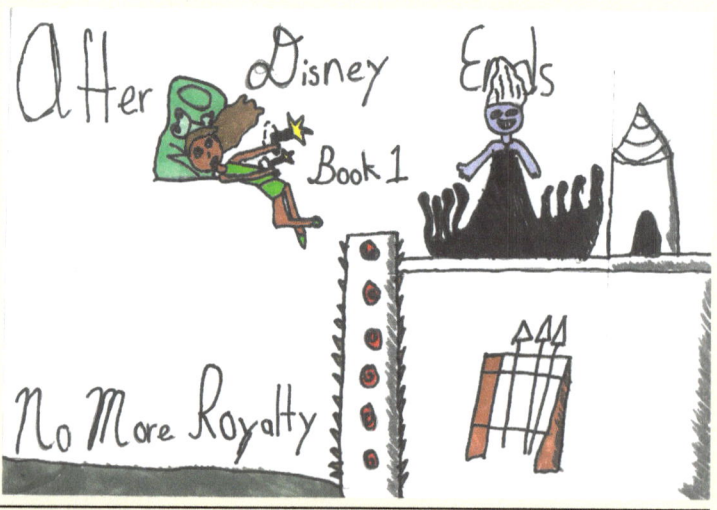

HOLLECKER, BETHENY
Tulsa, Oklahoma

HOLLECKER, DANIELLE
Tulsa, Oklahoma

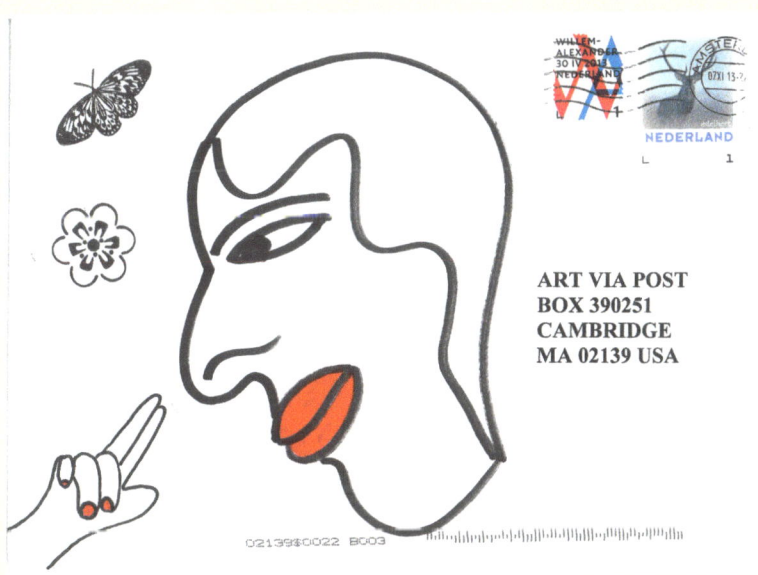

ART VIA POST
BOX 390251
CAMBRIDGE
MA 02139 USA

02139$0022 B003

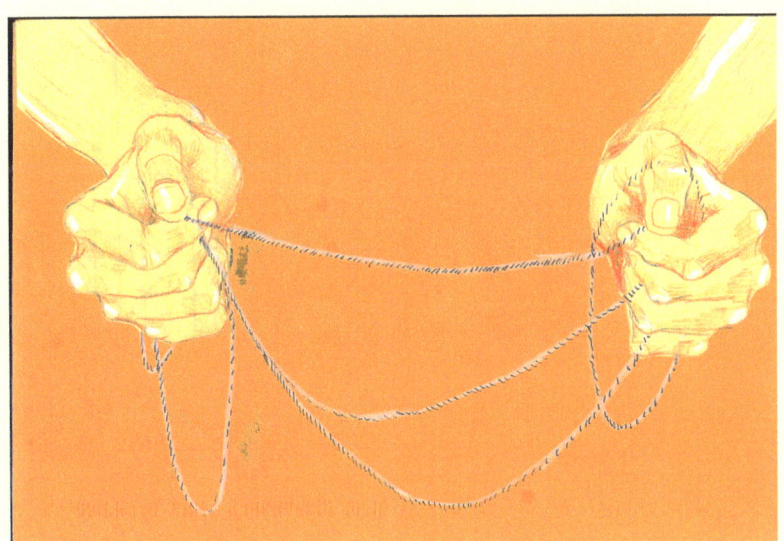

BUWS, RENEE

Holland

SHEA, BRENDAN

Abington, Massachusetts

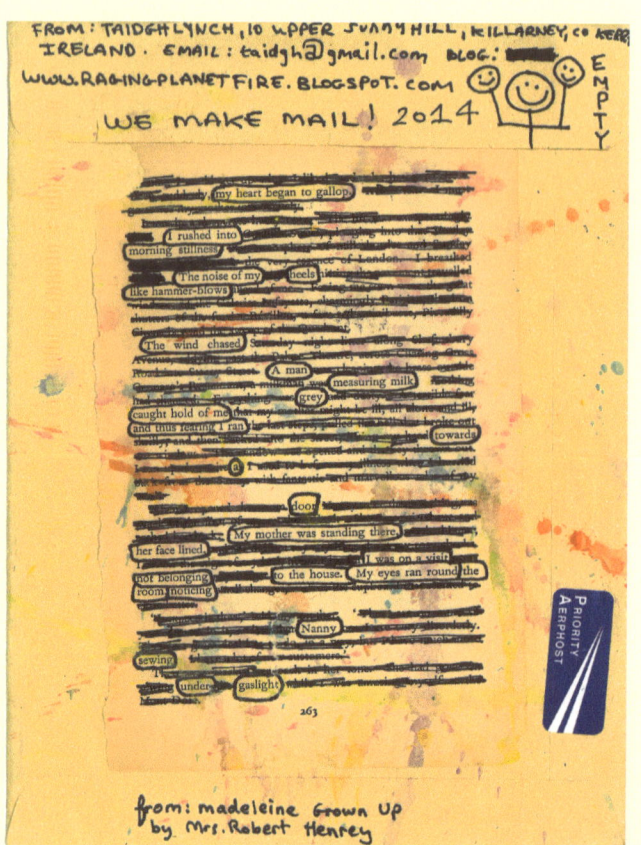

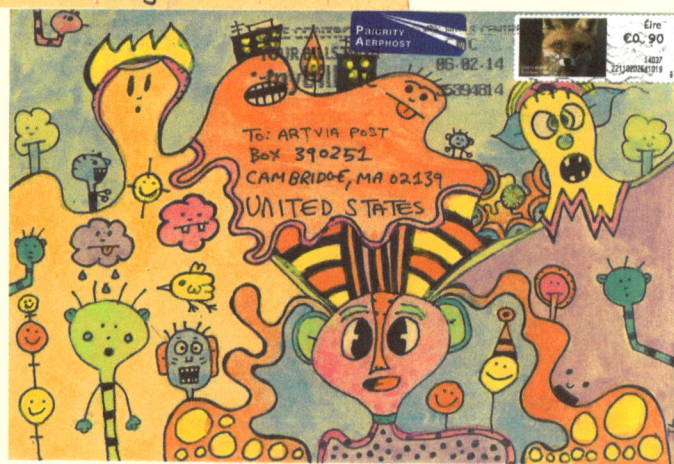

LYNCH, TAIDGH

Ireland

ragingplanetfire.blogspot.com

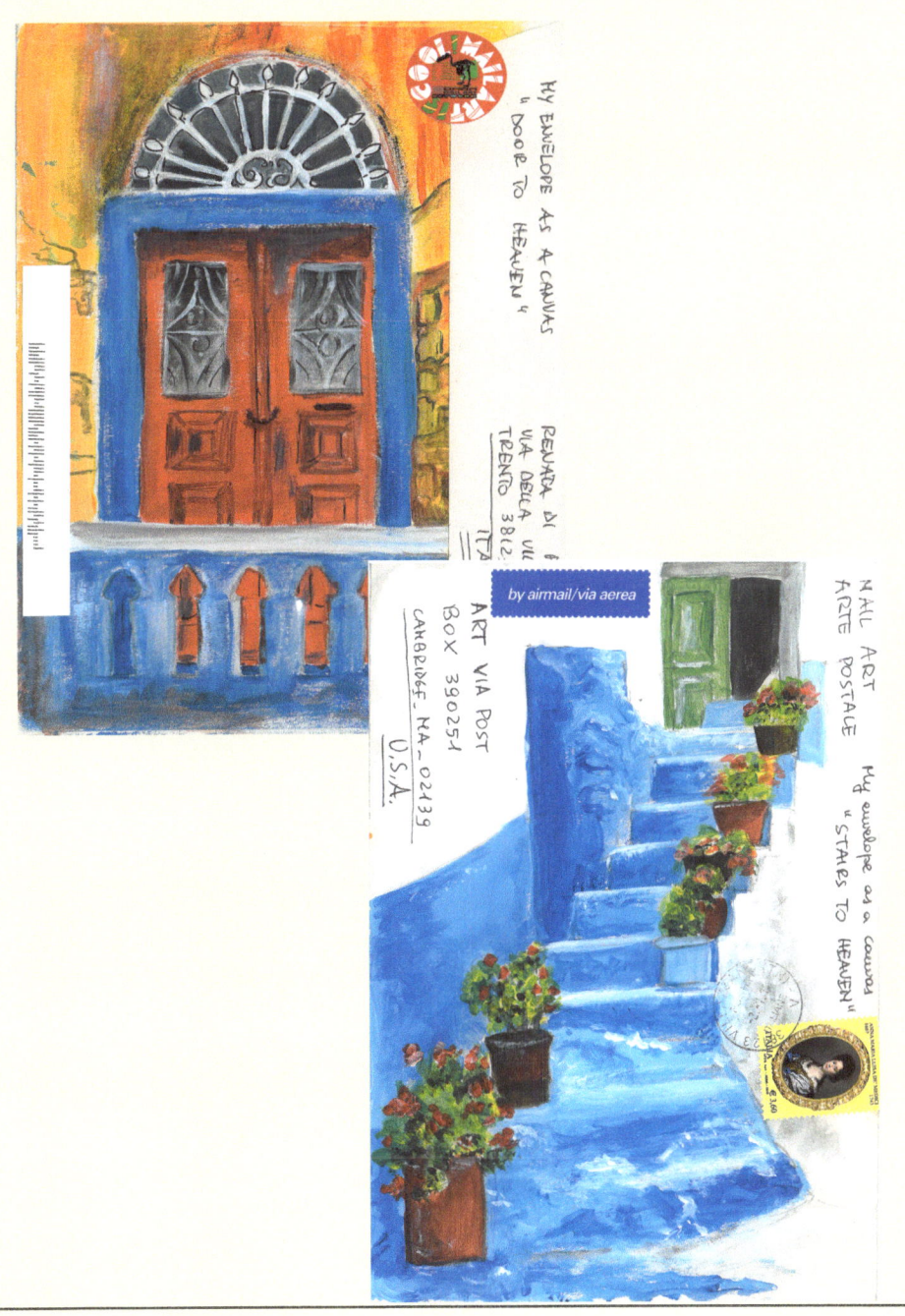

MY ENVELOPE AS A CANVAS
" DOOR TO HEAVEN "

RENATA DI
VIA DELLA VI
TRENTO 3812.
ITA

MAIL ART
ARTE POSTALE

MY envelope as a canvas
" STAIRS TO HEAVEN "

by airmail/via aerea

MAIL ART VIA POST
BOX 390254
CAMBRIDGE, MA 02139
U.S.A.

DI PALMA, RENATA

Italy

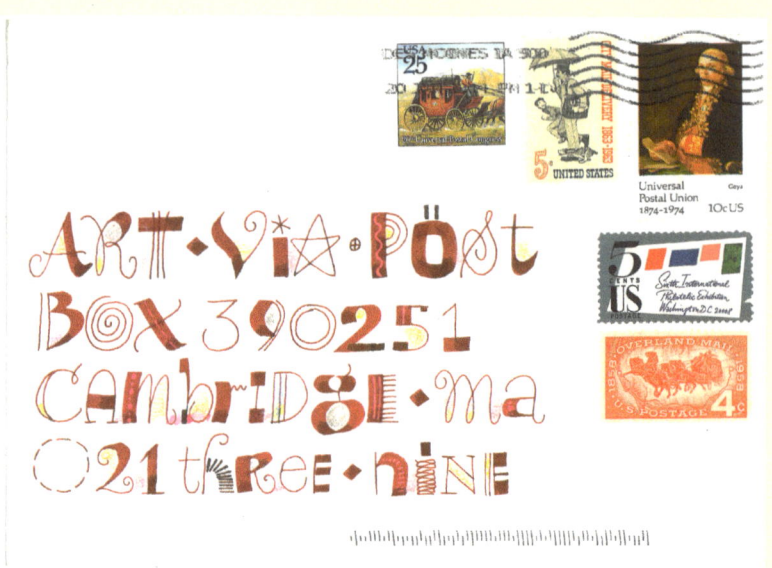

"I create mail art because (A) it is a quick and easy outlet for my creative juices (B) it is a way to offer online lessons - at my blog - (C)I regularly hear from my blog readers who are thrilled that they have found an artistic outlet and they ask me to keep posting my daily envelopes, which I have been doing since Feb 17, 2010. I have not missed a single day. I was inspired to submit to Art via Post because it seems like a good fit with my mission to publicize mail art as an art form that is welcoming to people of all ages with any kind of art background (or even no art back ground.)" - Jean Wilson

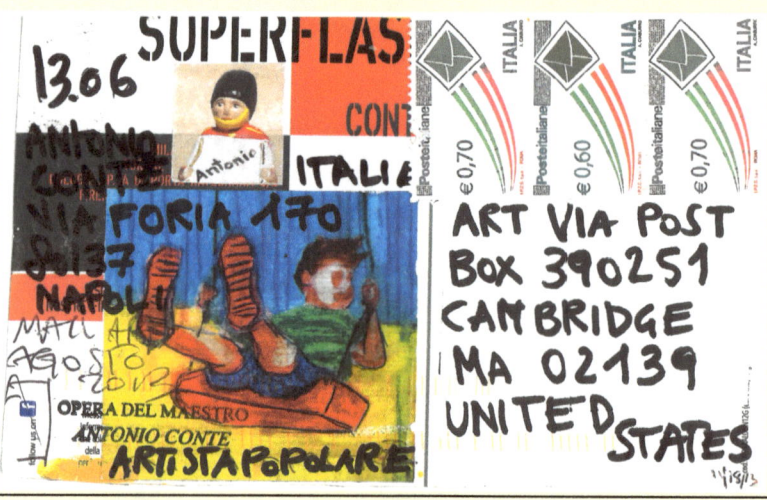

WILSON, JEAN

Des Moines, Iowa

pushingtheenvelopes.blogspot.com

CONTE, ANTONIO

Naples, Italy

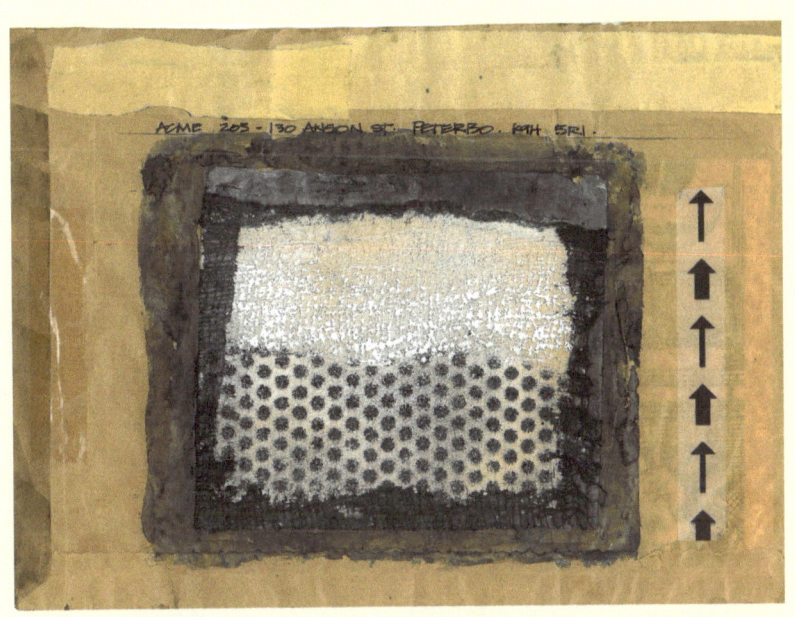

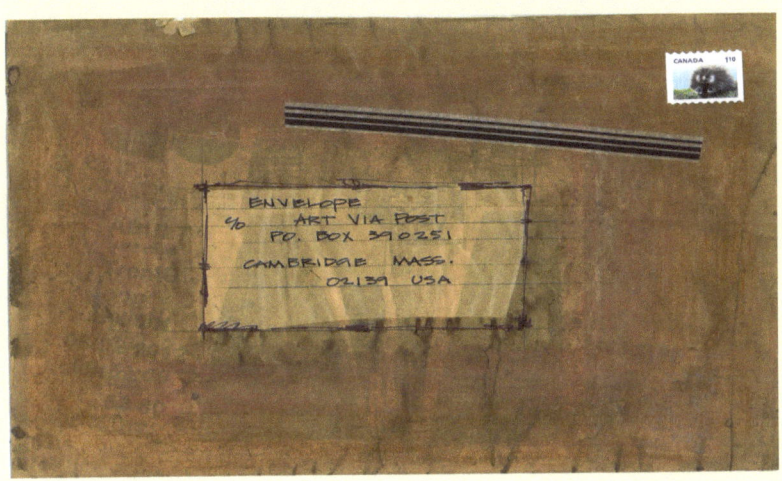

BAKER, (ACME)

Canada

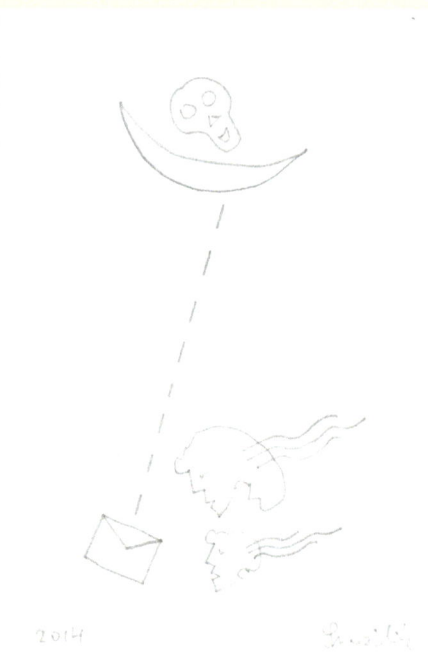

"Mail art is my skechbook with meaning." - Jaromir Svozilik

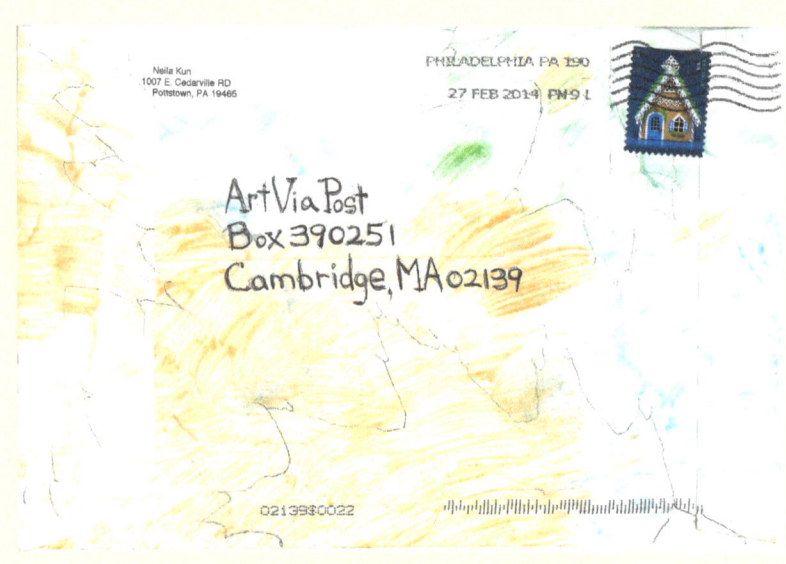

SVOZILIK, JAROMIR

Norway

svozilik.com

KUN, NEILA

Pottstown, Pennsylvania

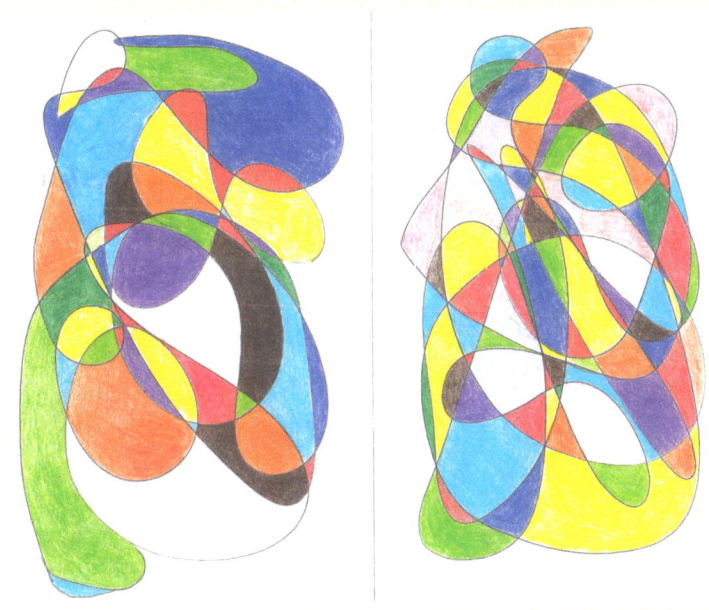

DENDLER, DEBORAH

Newton, Massachusetts

DeborahDendler.com

DEBIAGI, CONSUELO MARGARIDA R.

Brazil

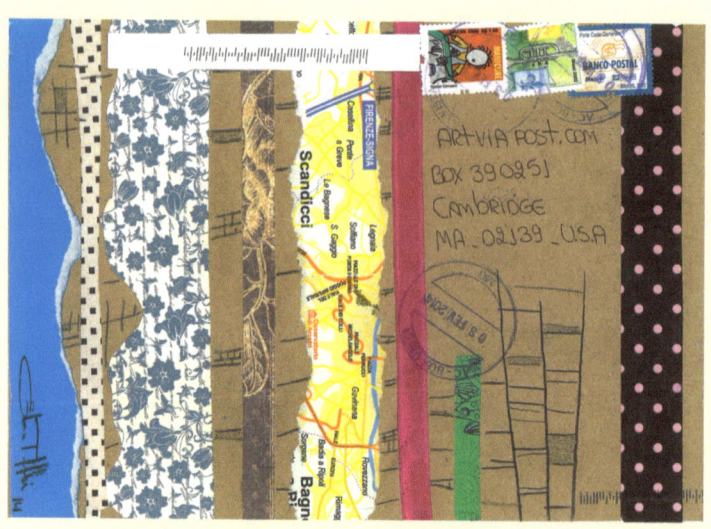

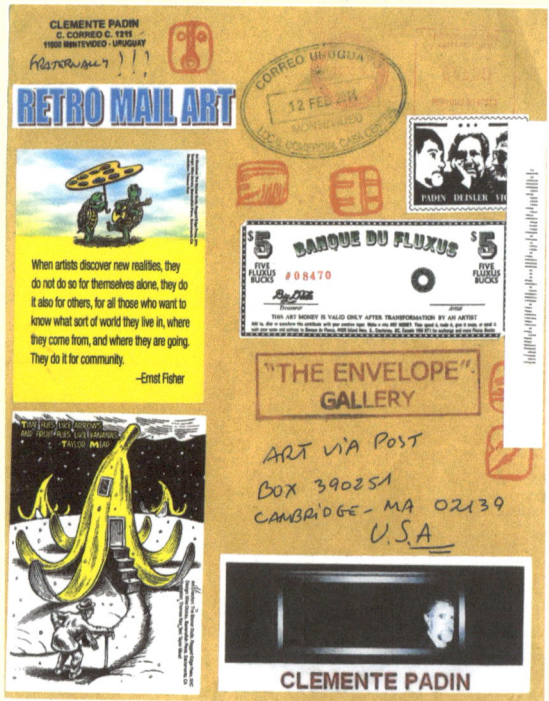

TOFFOLI, EDNA

Brazil

SPADIN, CLEMENTE

Uruguay

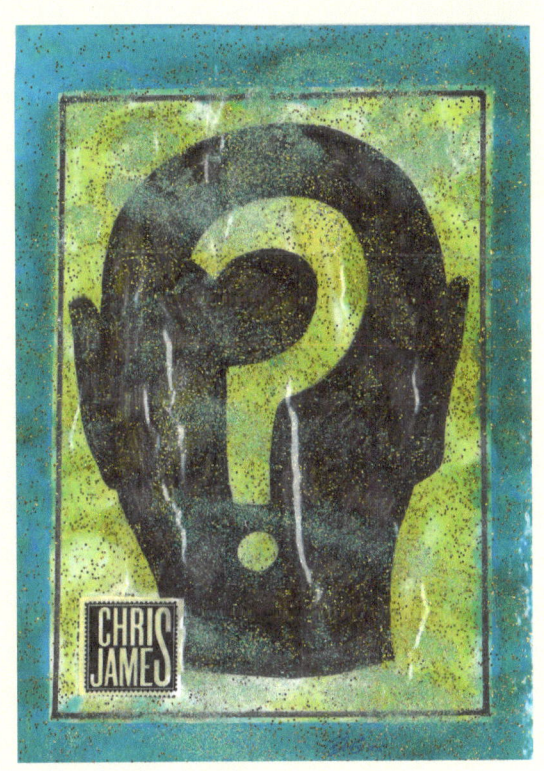

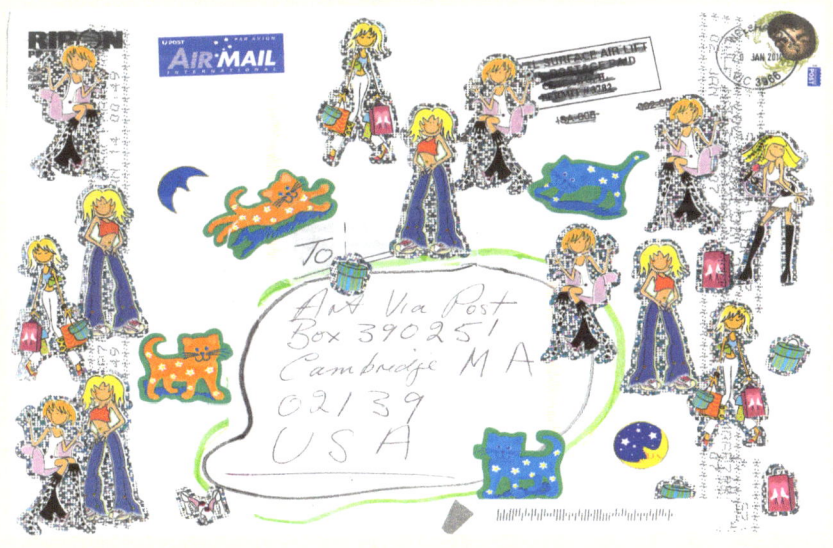

JAMES, CHRIS DR.

Victoria, Austraila

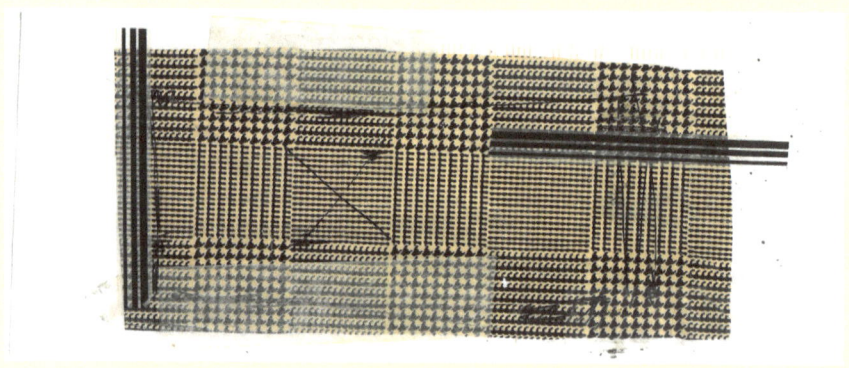

UNKNOWN

Canada

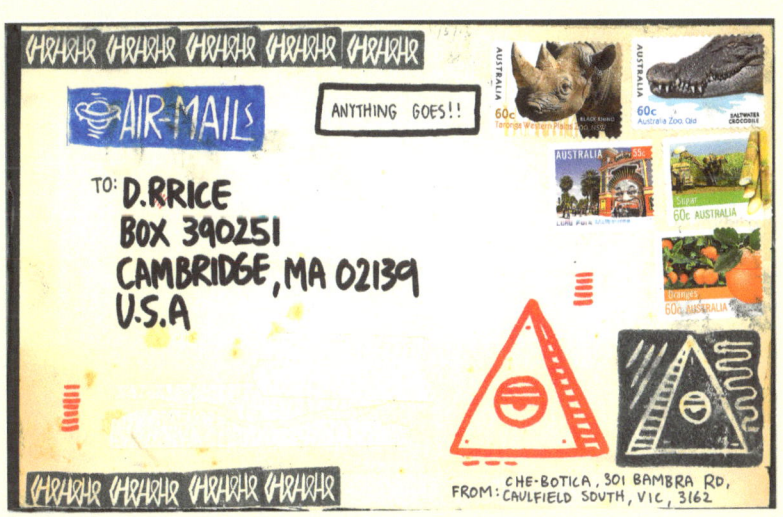

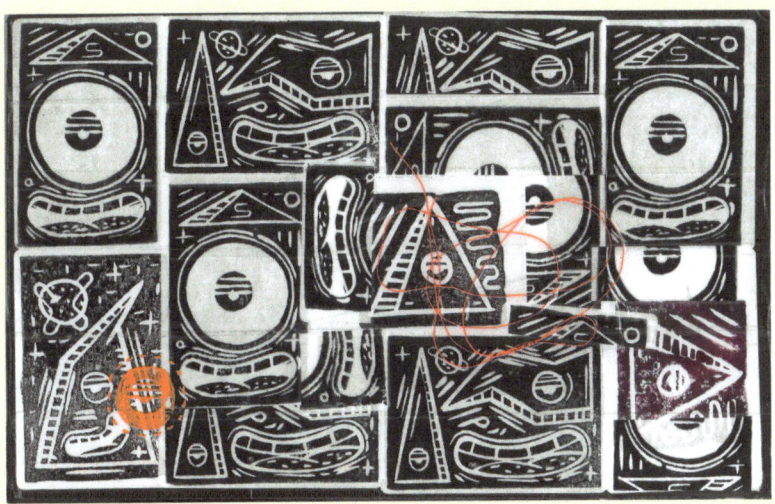

CHE-BOTICA

Australia

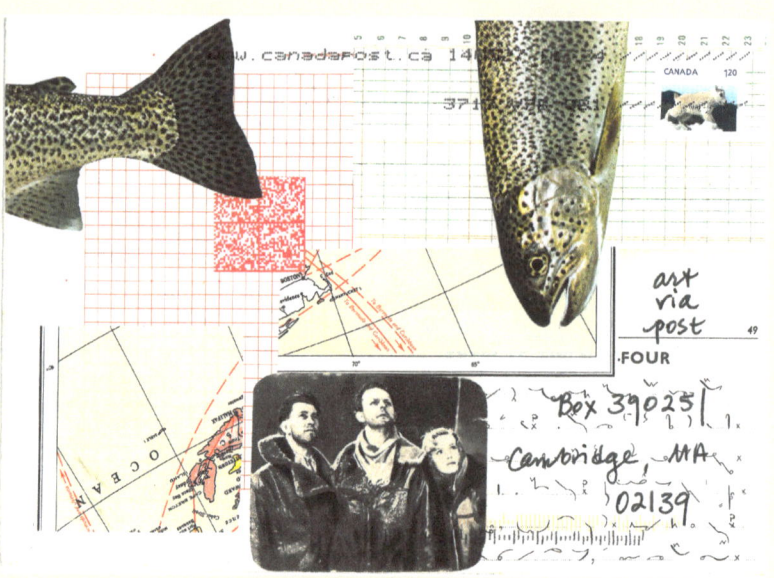

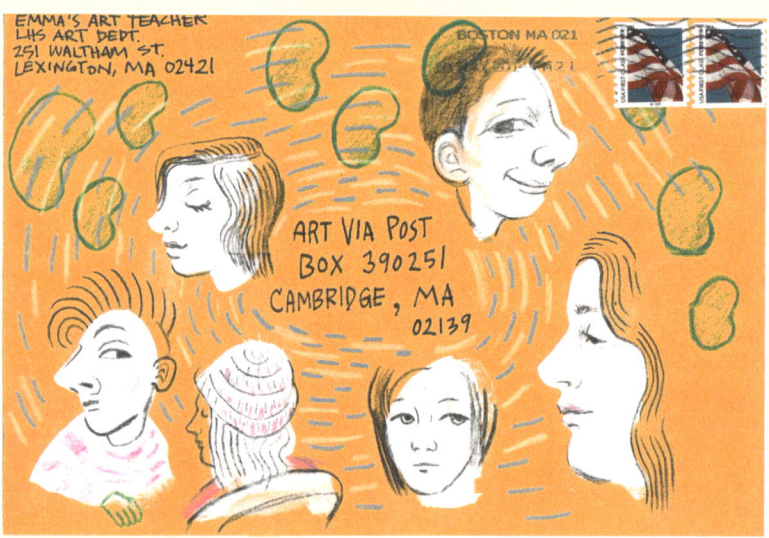

MASON, ADRIENNE

Canada

Toughcitywriter.blogspot.ca

BEAN, MS.

Lexington, Massachusetts

badgigi.com

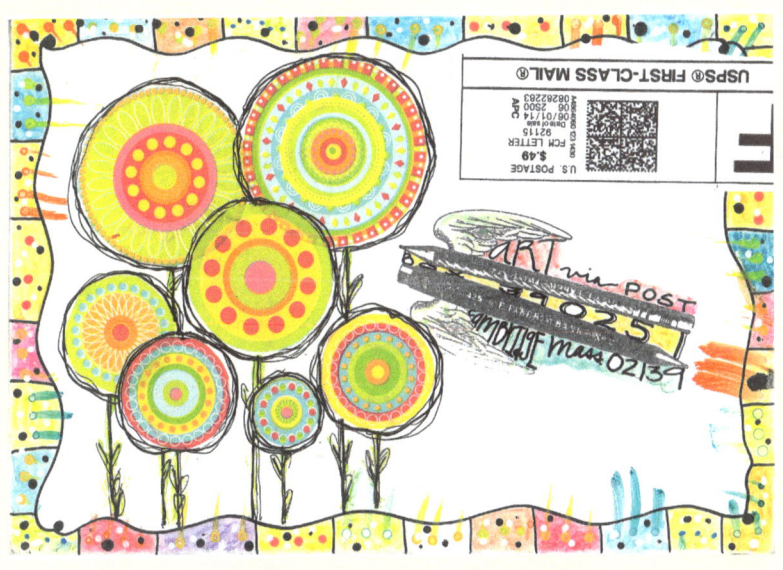

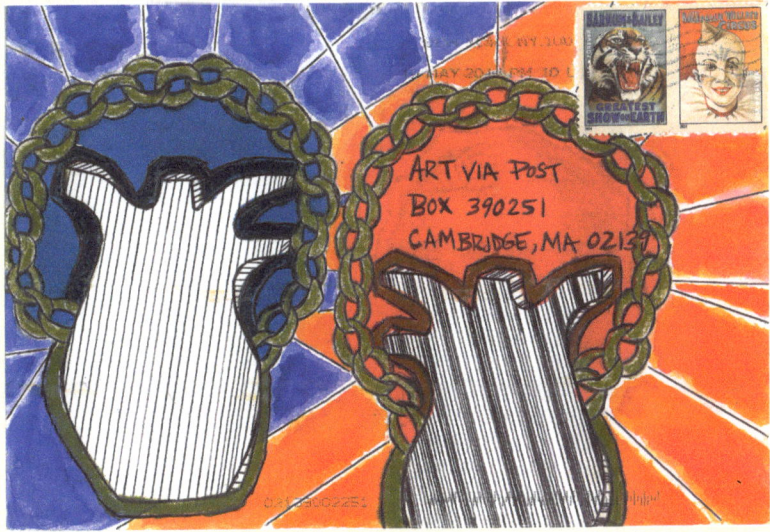

"I am fascinated by all things antiquated weither it be process or product. I see the mail system as becoming obsolete in my lifetime. Thus making it seen as a thing of the past. This call for mail art had intention and purpose which is the way I wish to create all my work."

- Sean Paul Gallegos

COYLE, JACKIE

San Diego, California

GALLEGOS, SEAN PAUL

Bronx, New York

seanpaulgallegos.com

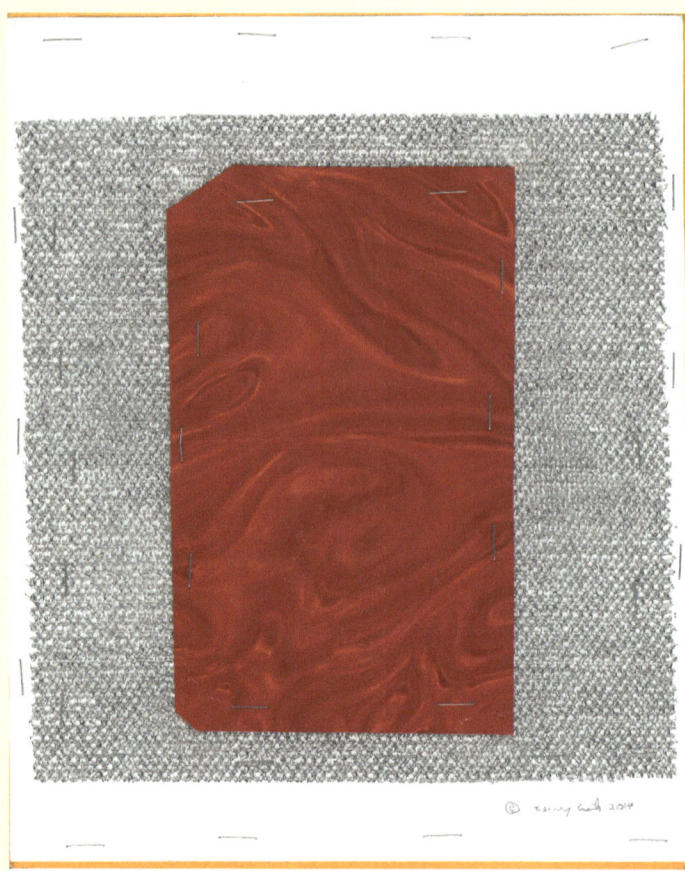

"I enjoy mail art because: I can create on a less formal basis with mailing materials and art materials that I have on hand; I enjoy making and sending the mail art; and hopefully someone will get to enjoy my creation on the other end, after it is mailed, and get some happiness.

Mail art is accessible to all and fun to do. Who knows, it may even brighten the day of the postal carrier transporting it. For me mail art also partly stems from a life-long enjoyment of going to the post office. I used to be a stamp collector when I was young. Now I am an artist. Mail art ties the two together nicely in a fun, creative way. I submitted to Art Via Post because it was going across the country, from Oregon to Massachusetts, which made it even more fun and interesting. In this case, although not all of my original mail art made it to Massachusetts enough of what I mailed survived to still make it fun and worthwhile."

- Lawrence Cwik

CWIK, LAWRENCE
Portland, Oregon

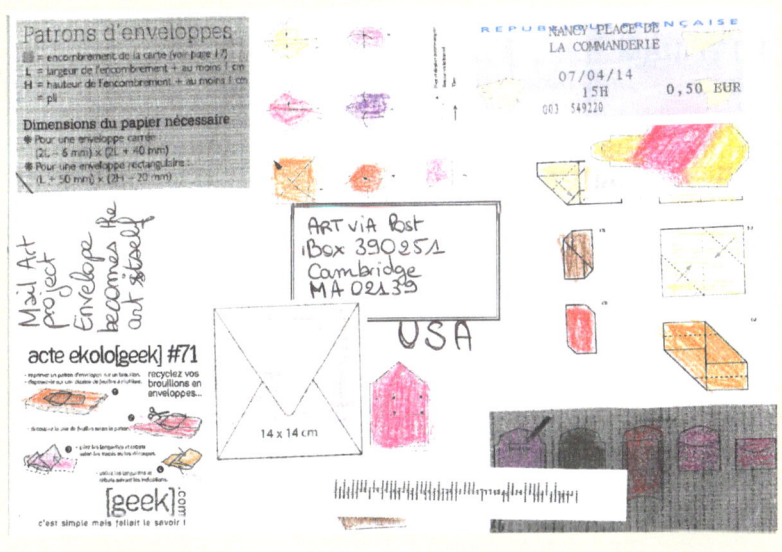

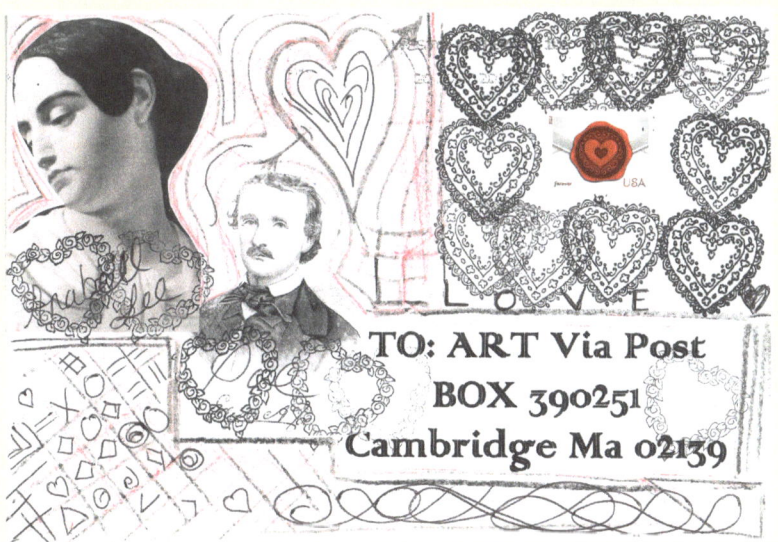

BOURJOT, JEANNE

France

MANCUSO, JOSPEH

Lake Peekskill, New York

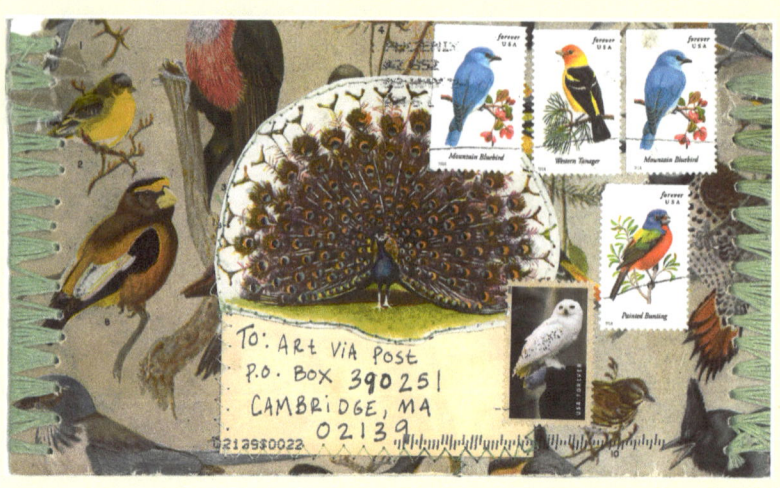

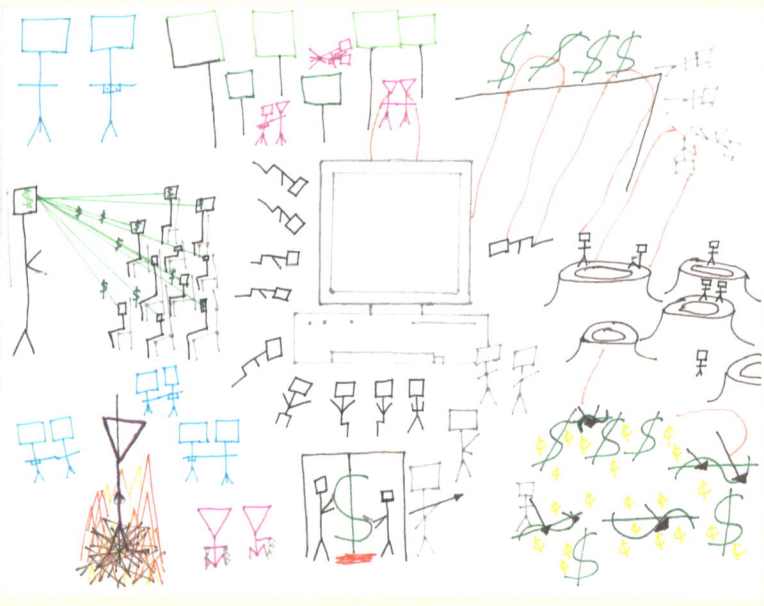

SPEECE, BILLIE JO

Phoenix, Arizona

HENRY, JON

Virginia

thejonhenry.com

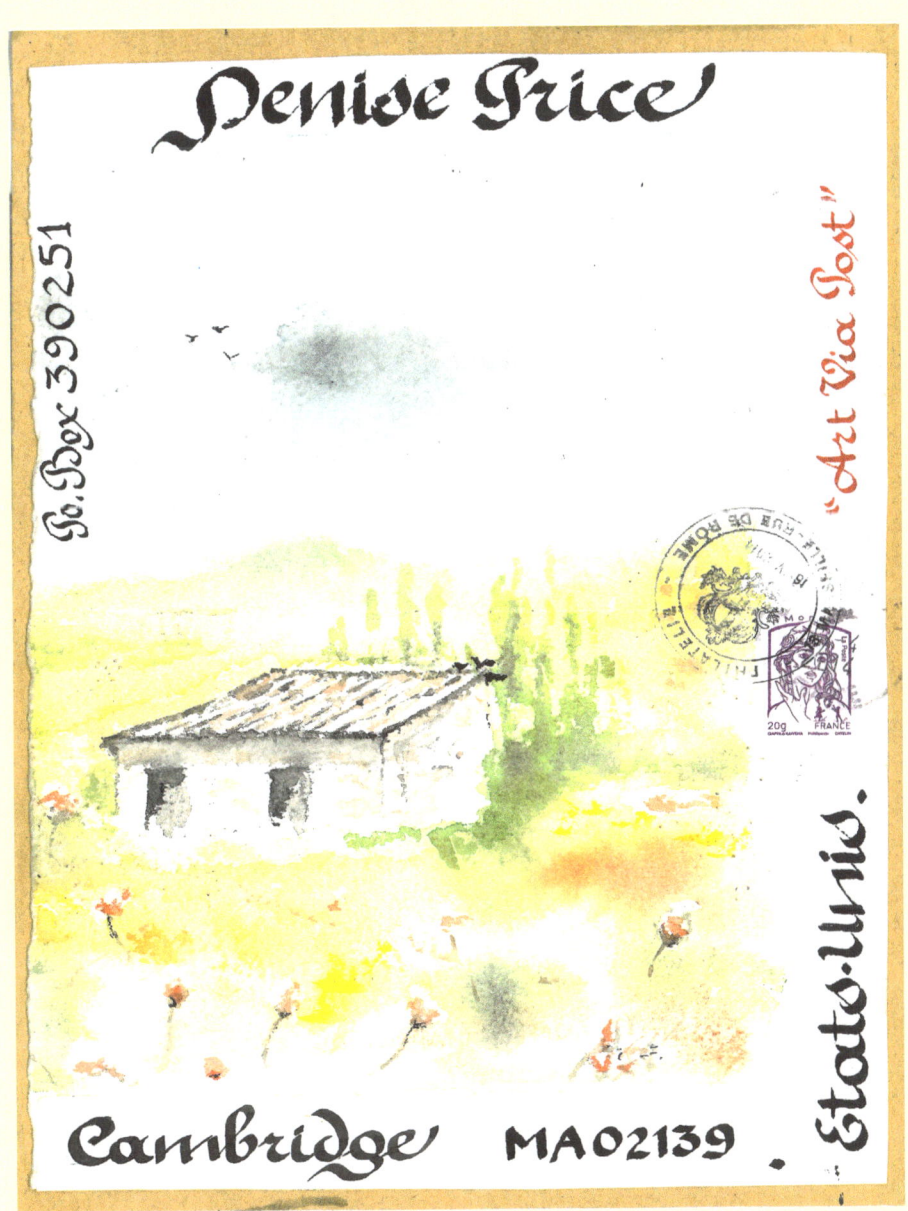

Denise Price

P.o.Box 390251

"Art Via Post"

20g FRANCE

Cambridge MA02139

Etats·Unis.

BAUDET, RICHARD

France

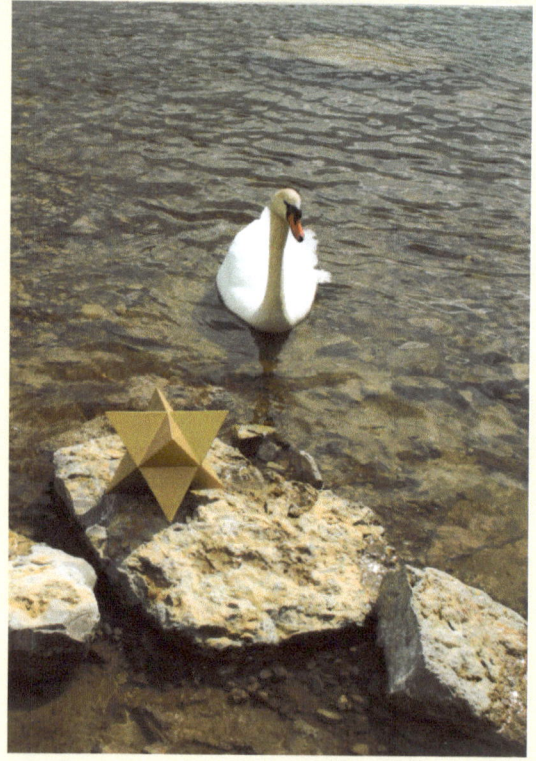

THORNTON, P.

Ontario, Canada

SCHMIDT, SANDRA SIMONE

Germany

dodeca-art.com

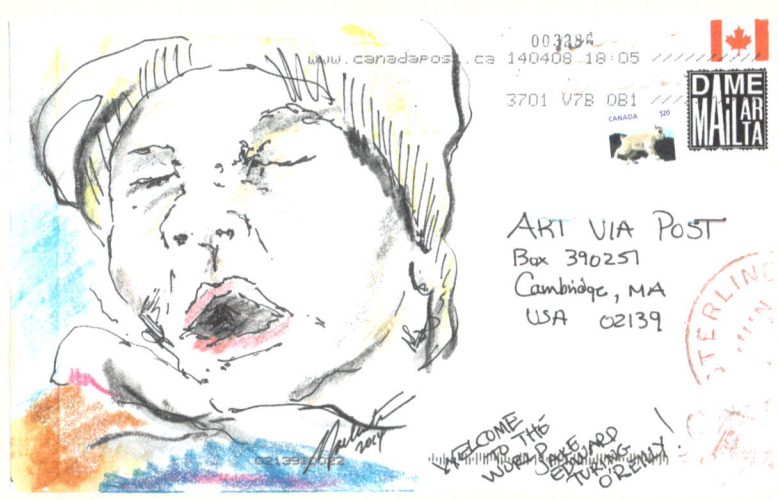

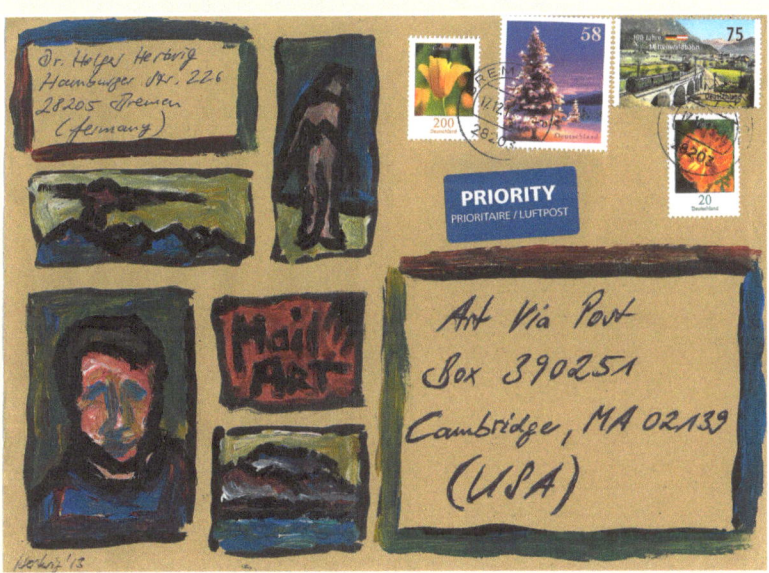

MAILARTA

Canada

HERTWIG, HOLGER

Germany

facebook: Holger Hertwig

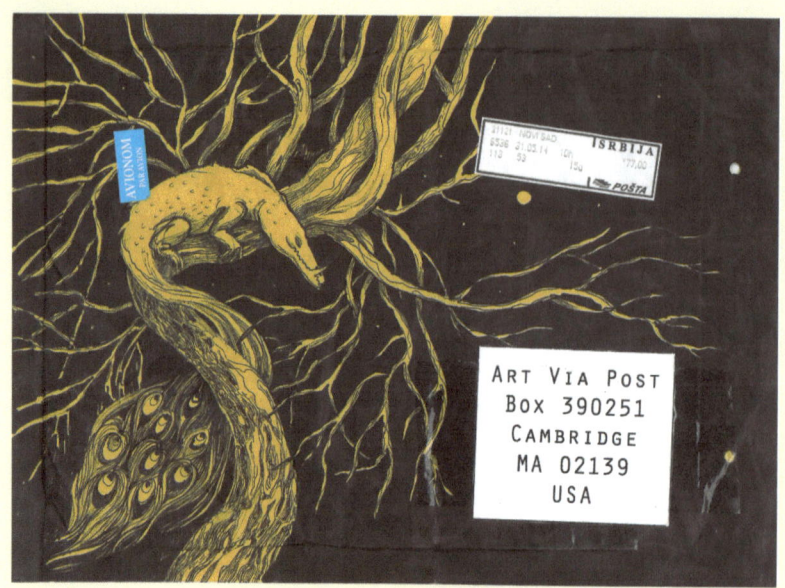

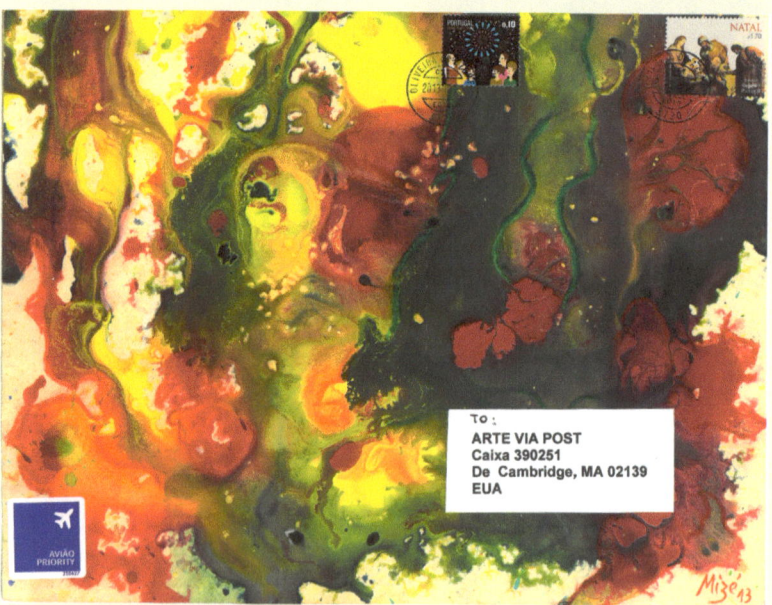

BRANOVACKI, DUNJA

Novi Sad, Serbia

AD1492.tumblr.com

SILVA-MIZE, MARIA JOSE

Portugal

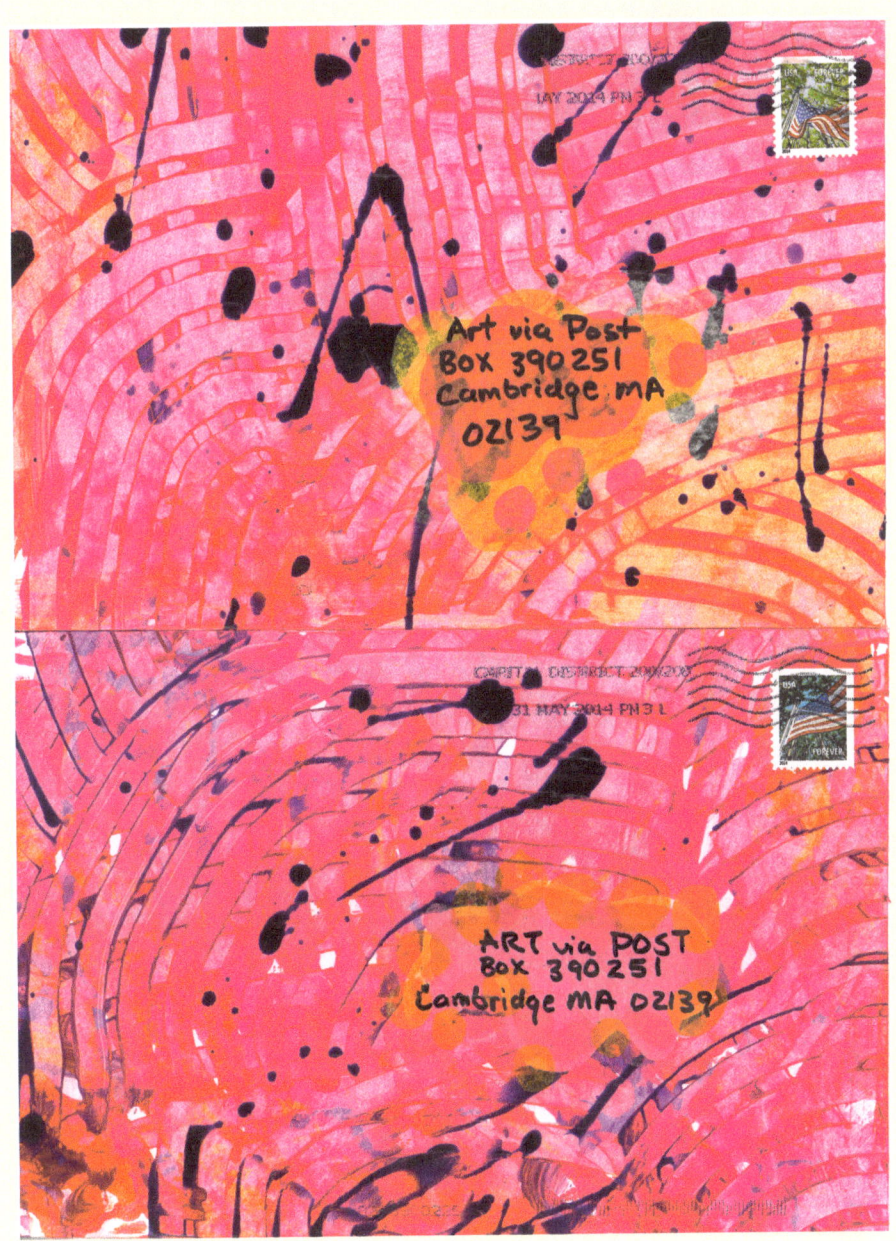

BURROWES, ADJOA J.

Maryland

ajoaburrowesfineart.com

Facebook: adja.burrowes

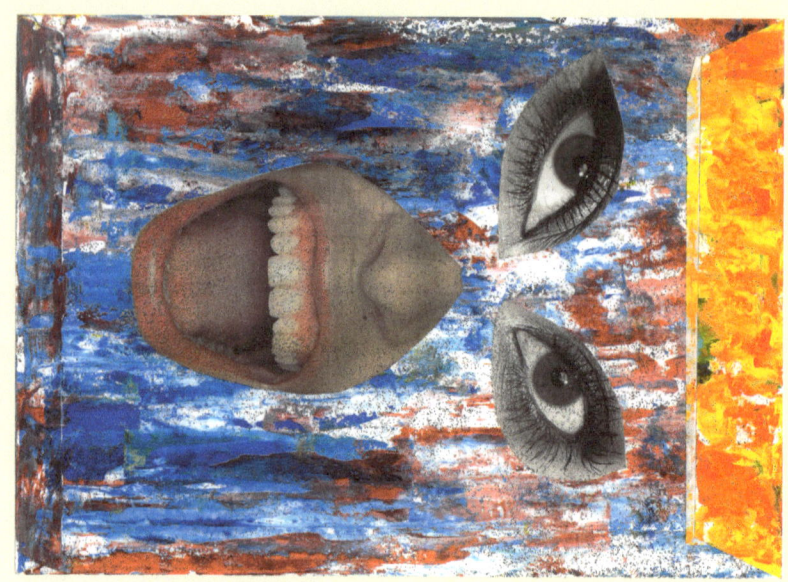

" I think mail art is the most fun way to spread love for art" - Ana Garcia

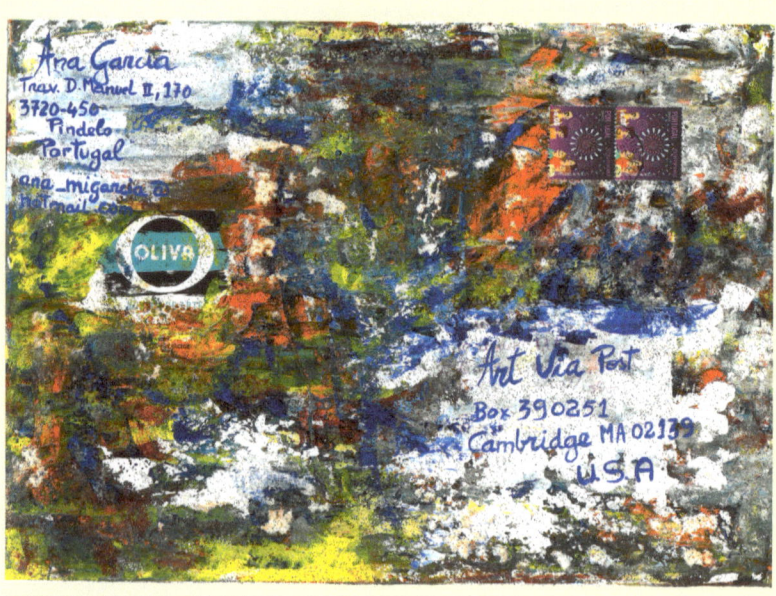

GARCIA, ANA

Portugal

iststwitterhandle

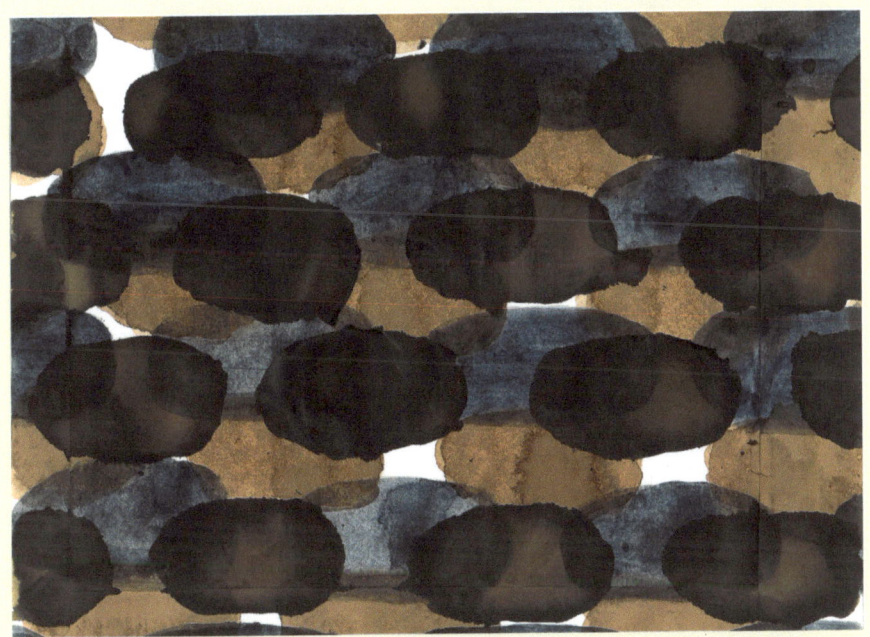

"I love being part of something so vast and so shared as Art via Post. Mail art has a long history, and it connects to many radical art movements like artist books, where artists reinvent a form in order to transform, challenge and 'consume' it in new ways. A friend sent me the invitation and I decided to paint on the envelope as I would on paper, with natural inks. I imagined it winging through the mail as a missive rather than a painting.."

- Sarah Sutro

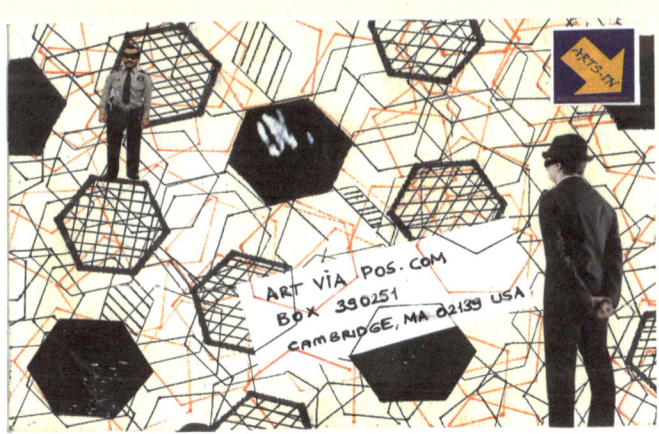

SUTRO, SARAH
North Adams, Massachusetts
sarahsutro.com

TURSOLUK, AILAL
Istanbul, Turkey
lebrix.com/milaltursoluk

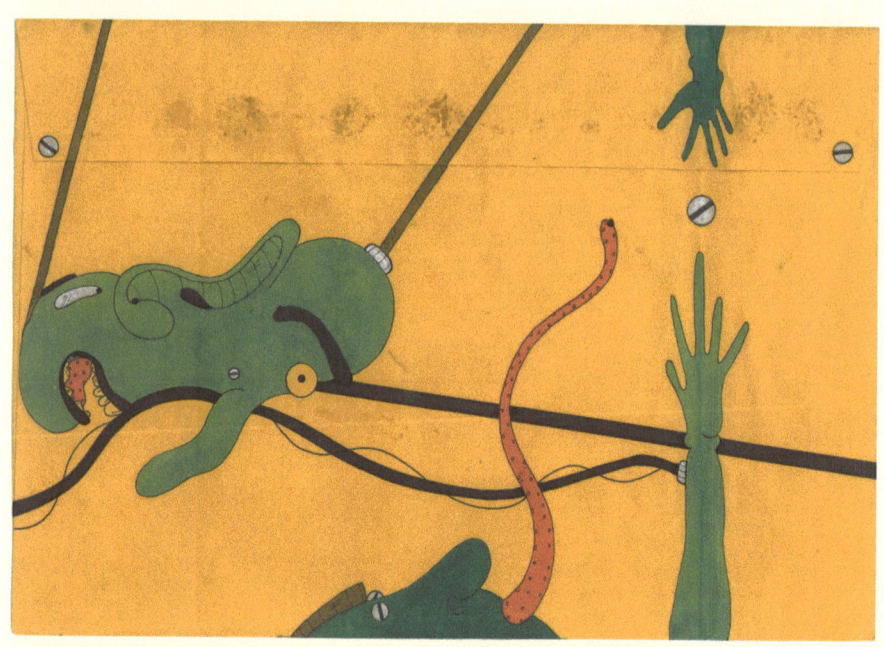

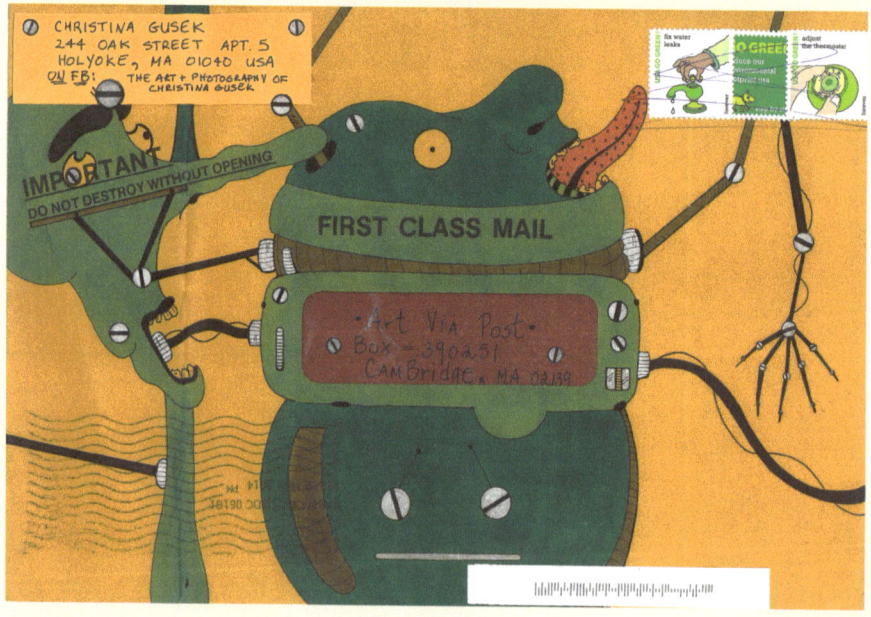

GUSEK, CHISTINA

Holyoke, Massachusetts

Facebook: The-Art-and-Photography-

of-Christina-Gusek

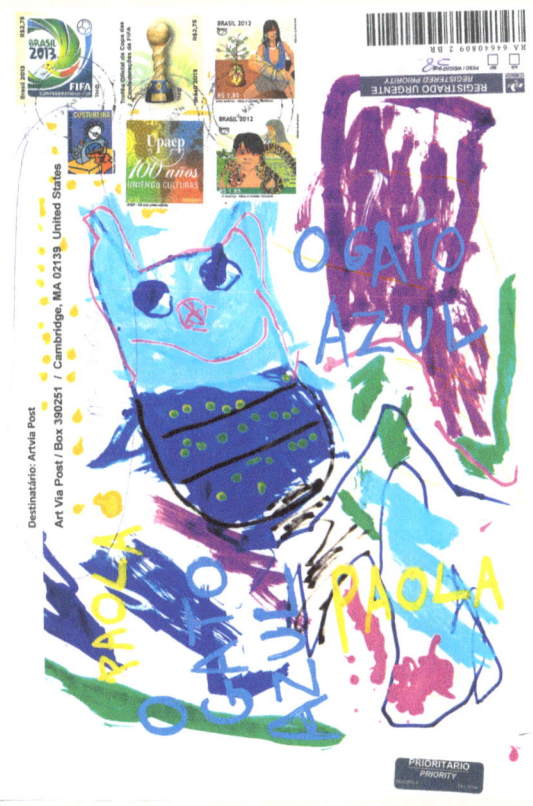

"This drawing was done by my daughter five years old. She drew a picture and gave it to me. When I asked why the cat was blue, she replied: "That kitten exists only in my imagination and in my imagination all that is blue is more beautiful So I drew it blue. . . " Loved the design and the explanation and decided to share with the world some-how." - As shared by her father, Fabiano Ignacio

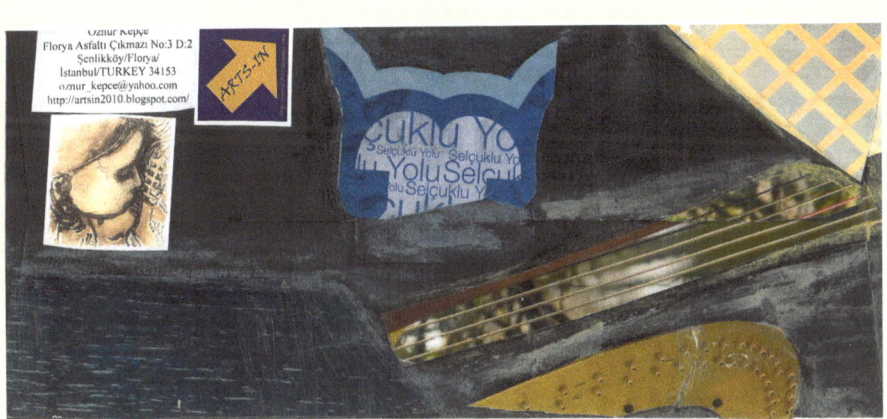

IGNACIO, PAOLA

Brazil

KEPCE, OZNUR

Istanbul, Turkey

artsin2010.blogspot.com

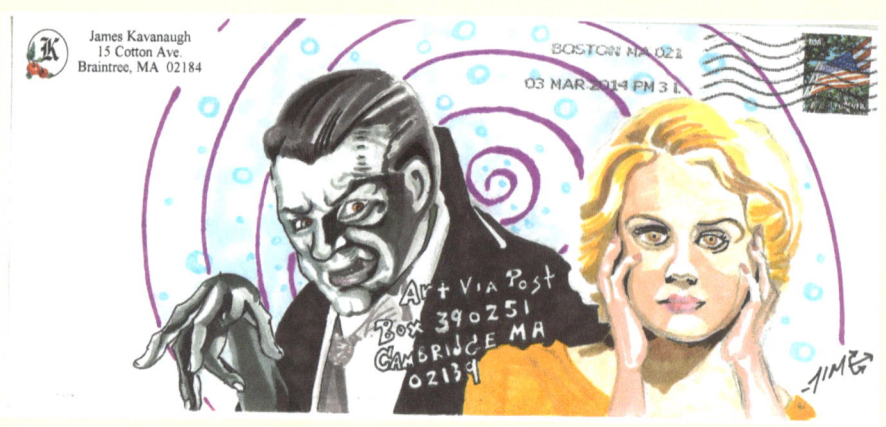

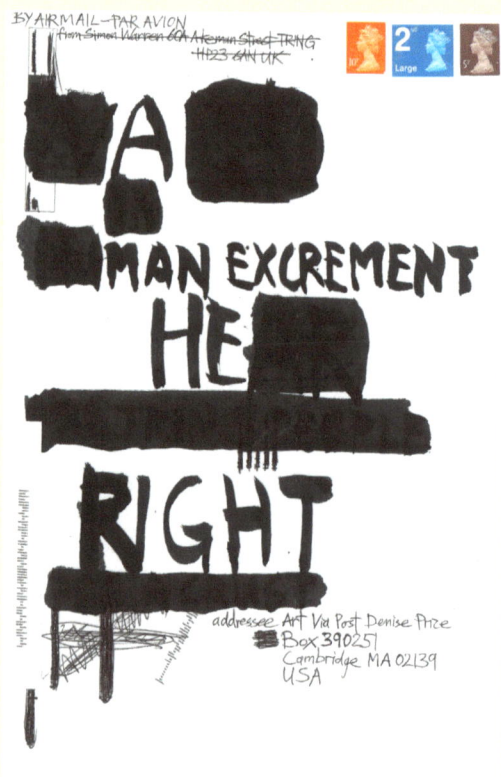

KAVANAUGH, JAMES

Braintree, Massachusetts

WARREN, SIMON

United Kingdom

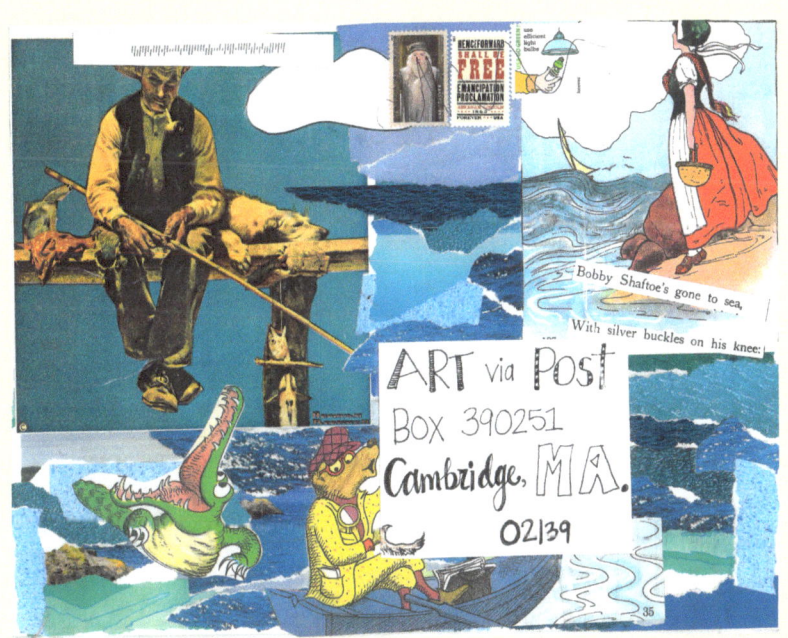

GLASS, THERESA

Grand Rapids, Michigan

Instagram: tgtglass

BAHAN, TIFFANY

Urbana, Ohio

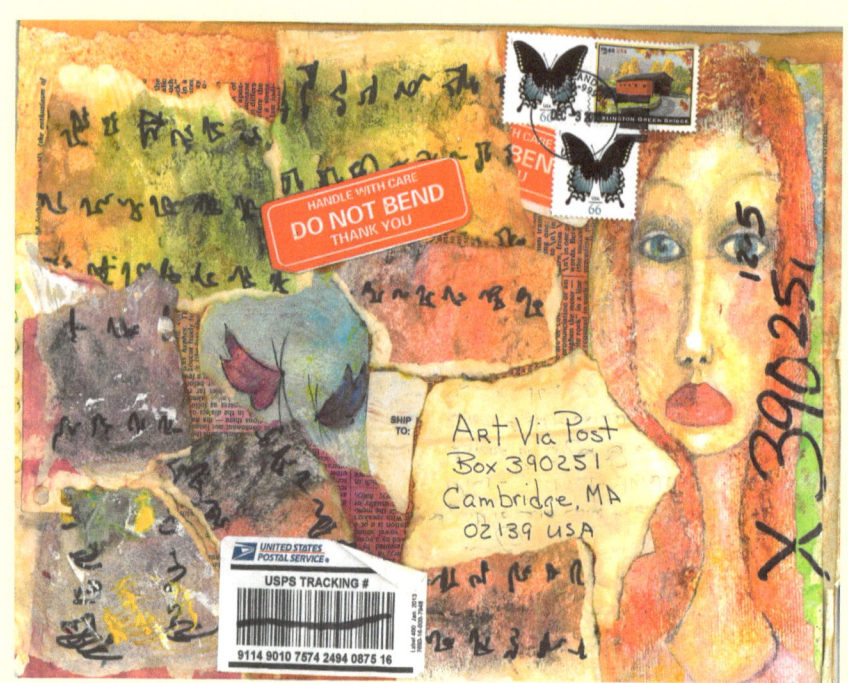

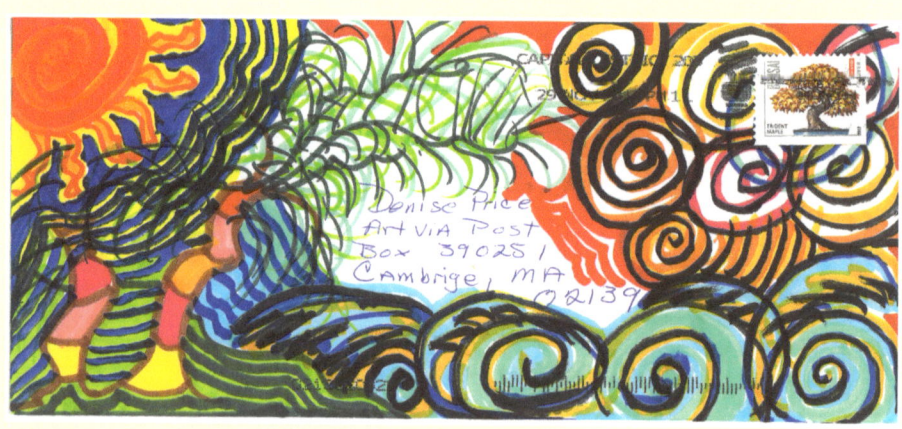

KOFFORD, BRENDA

Wheatland, Wyoming

ameditativejourney.wordpress.com

SKOLNICK, JUDY

Washington D.C.

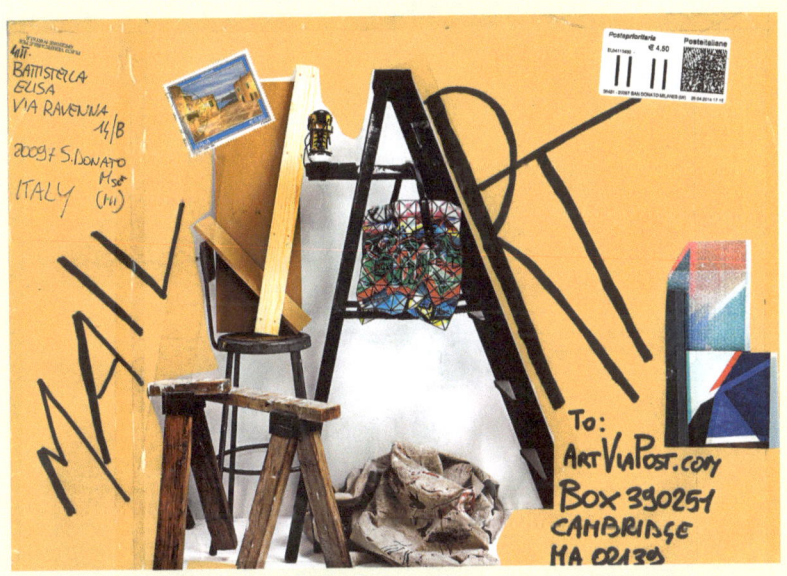

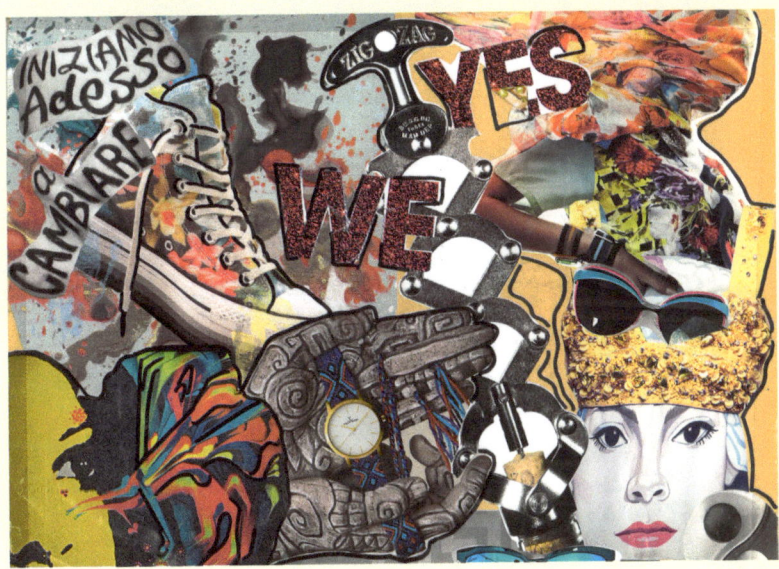

BATTISTELLA

Italy

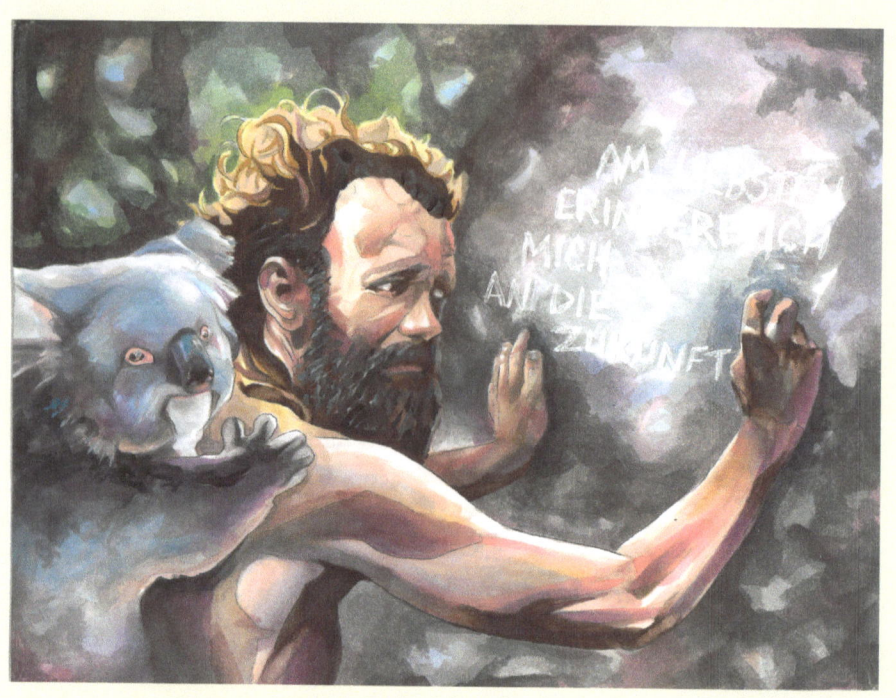

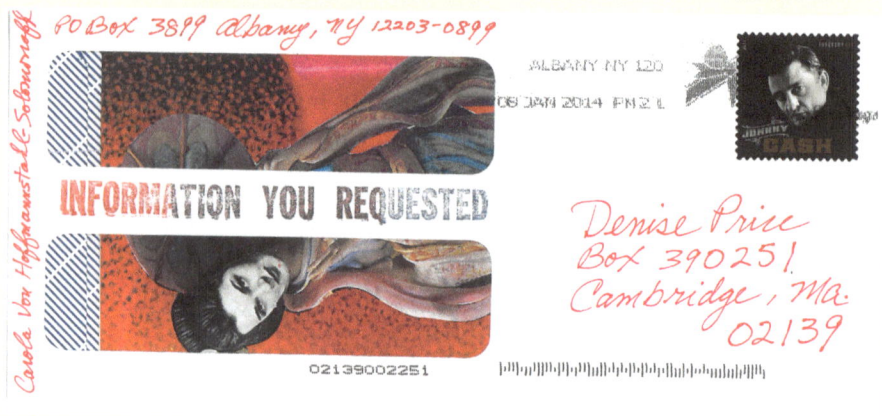

ELLISON, LUKE

Toledo, Ohio

lukeellison.com

VON HOFFMANSTAHL-SOLOMONOFF, CAROLA

Albany, New York

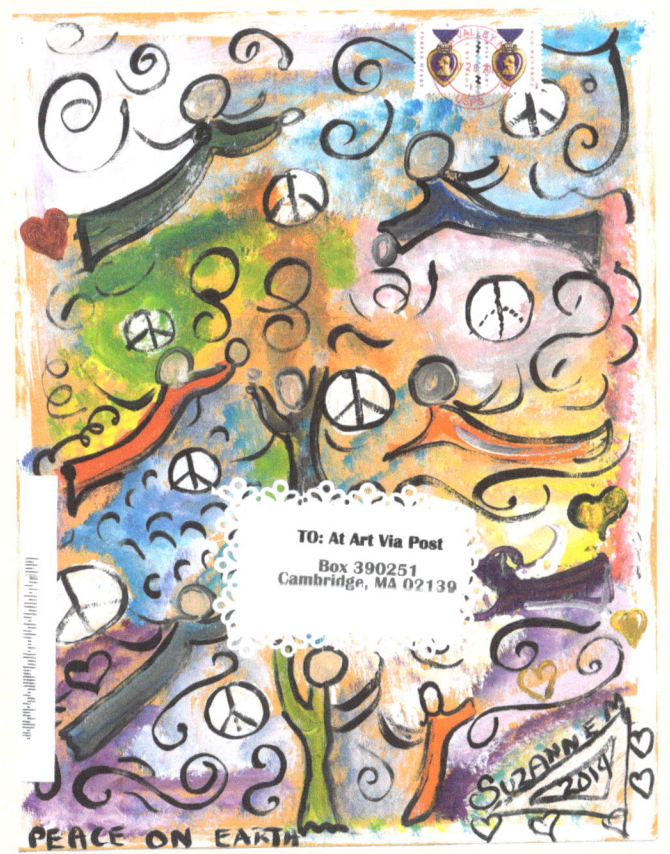

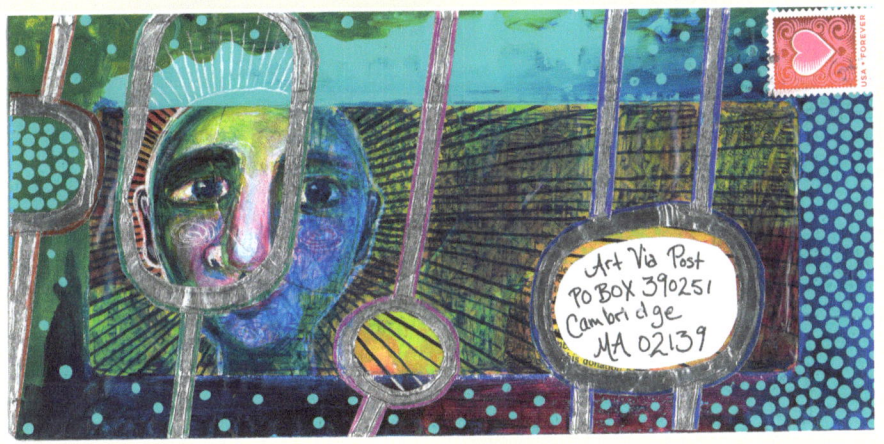

MANCUSO, SUZANNE KRAUS

Lake Peekskill, New York

Instagram @artistsinstragram

DAVIES, CARROLL

Wolcott, Vermont

Flicker: CarrollDavis/Bigmamabird

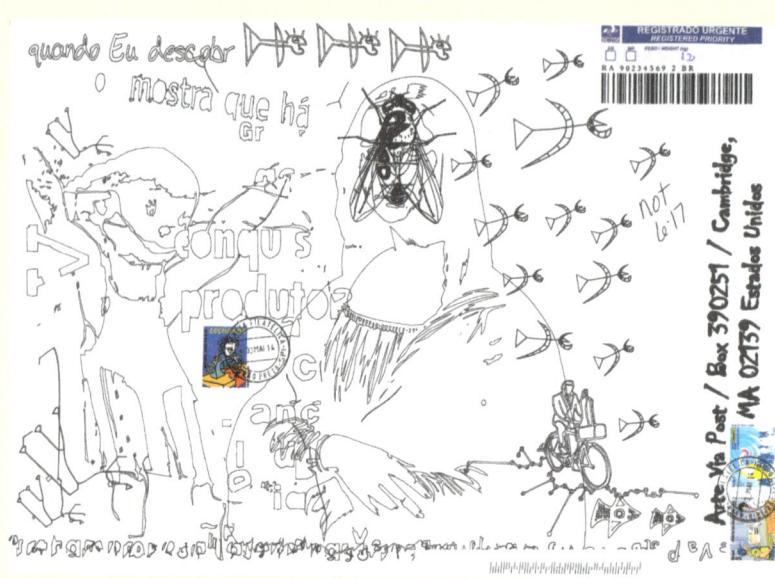

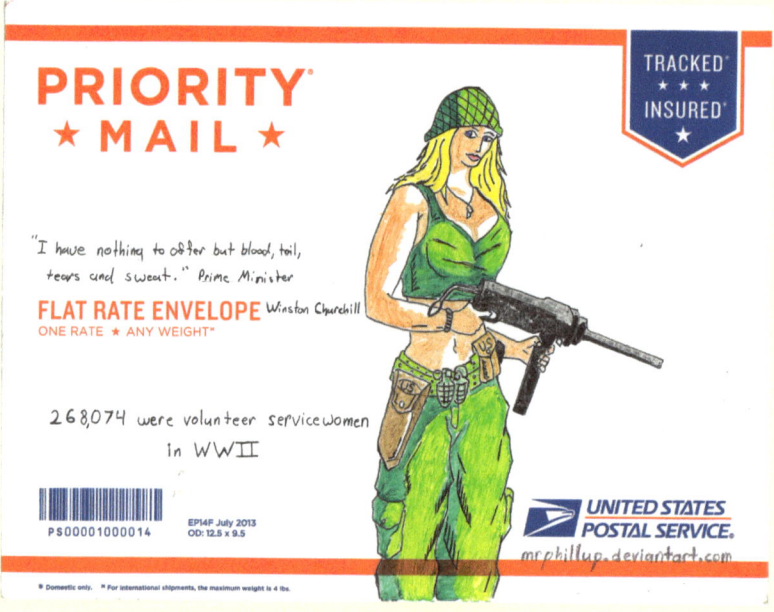

CORTA, ANDRE

Brazil

HOLLECKER, PHIL

Tulsa, Oklahoma

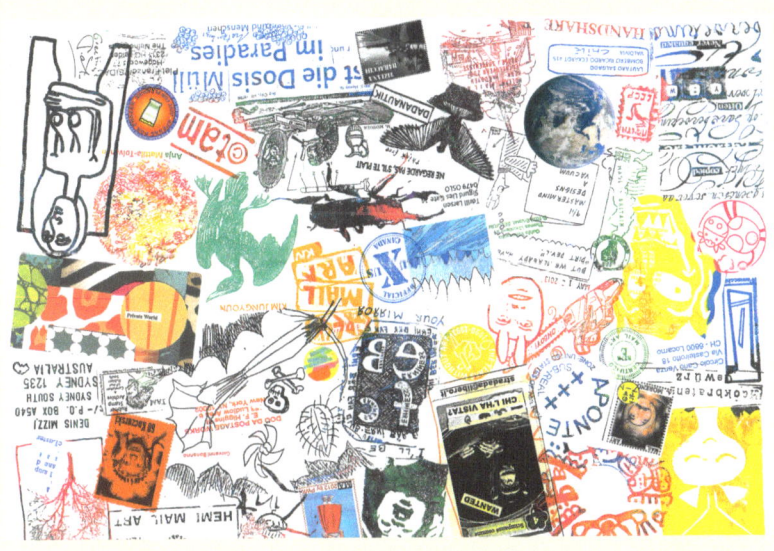

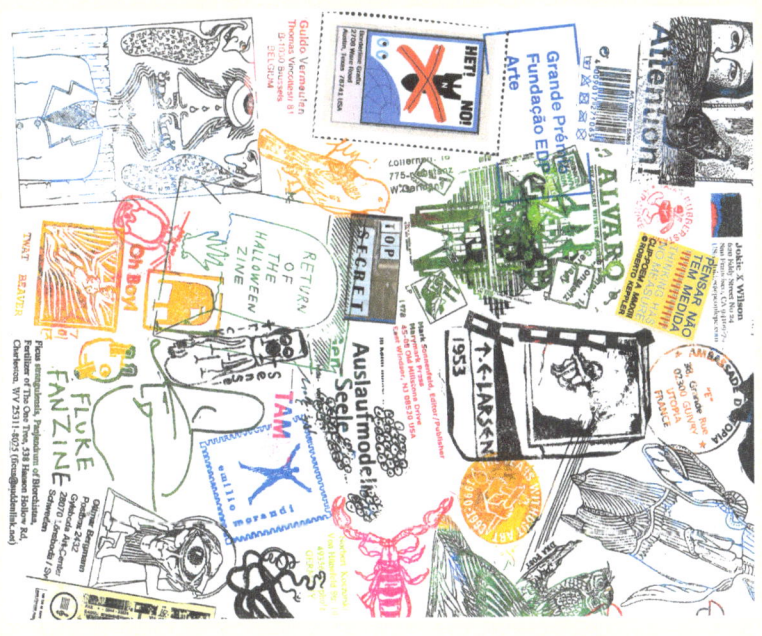

COHEN, RYOSUKE

Japan

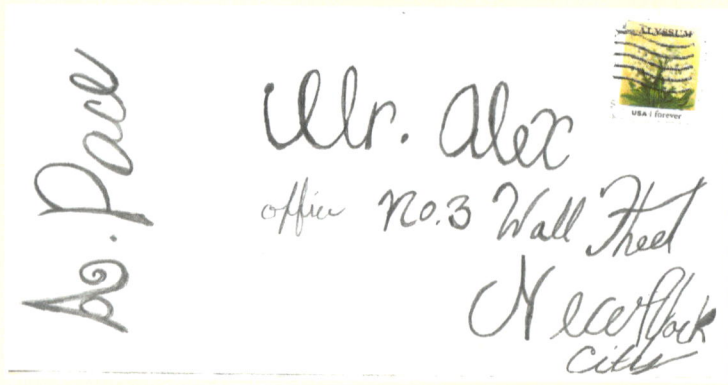

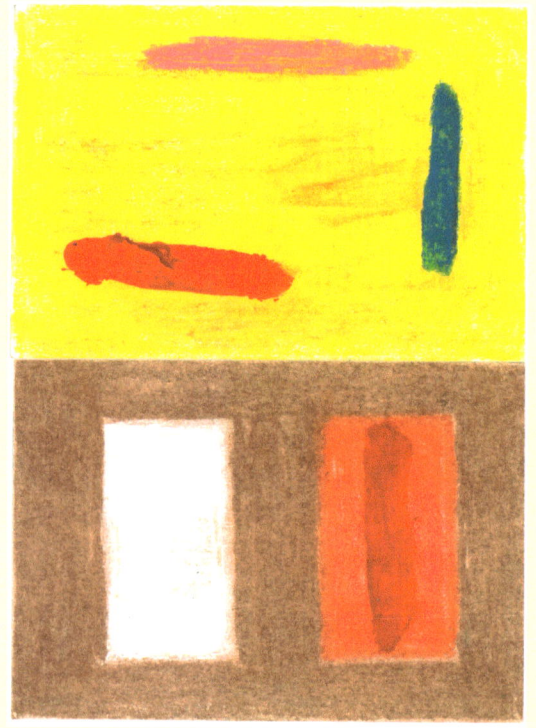

PACE, ANDRE

Phoenix, Arizona

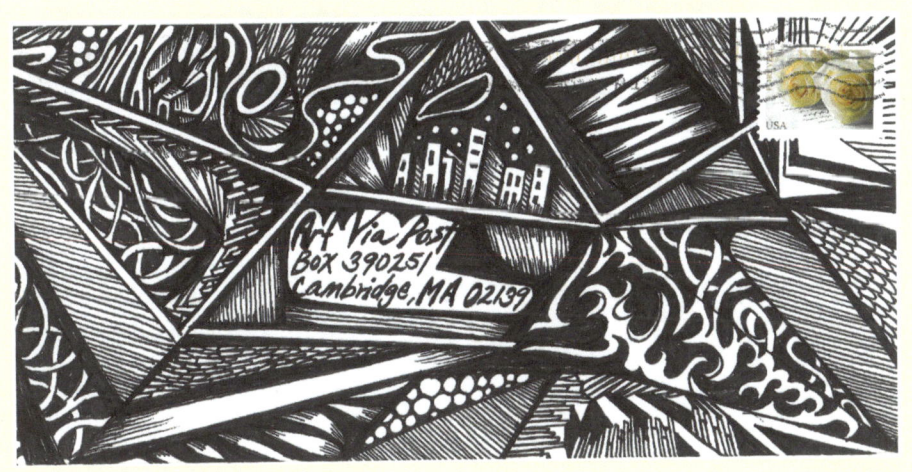

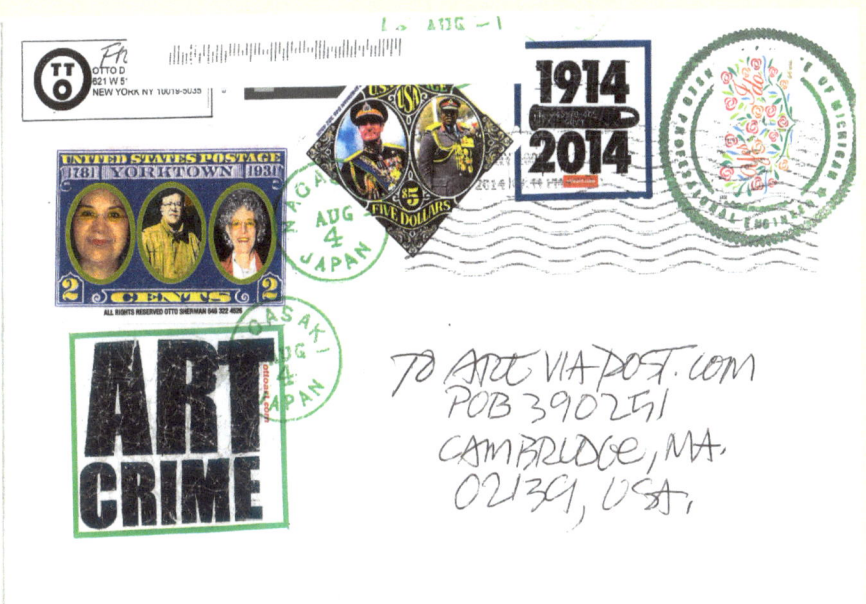

UNGER, KATY

Los Angeles, California

SHERMAN, OTTO

New York, New York

ottoart.com

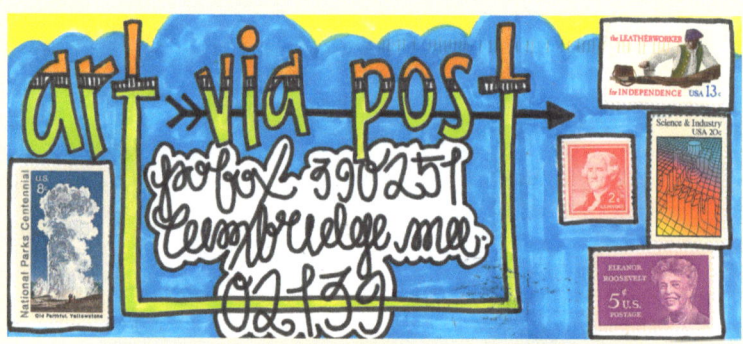

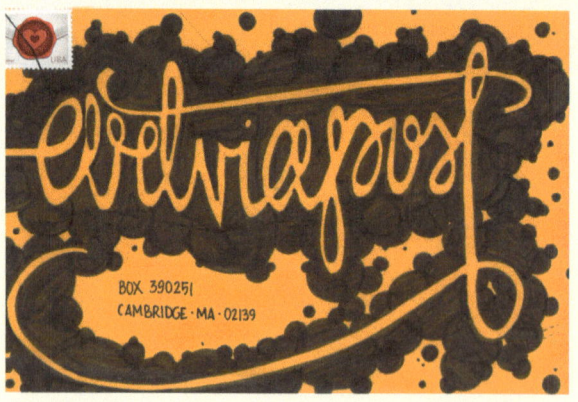

KATIE

Kent, Washington

maybekatie.com

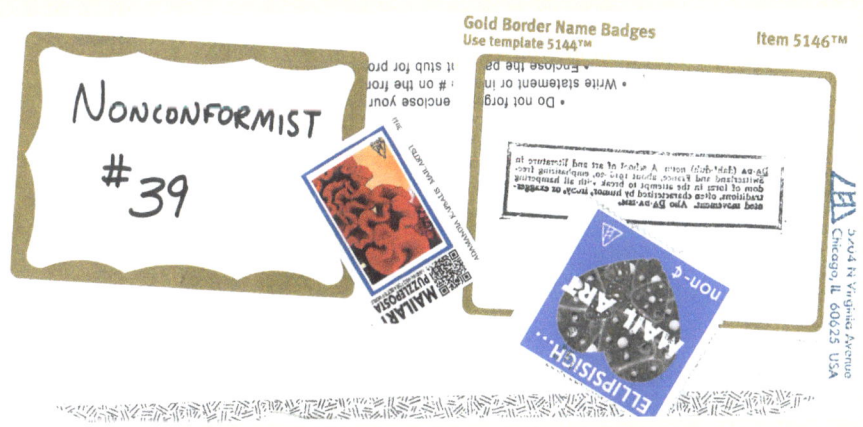

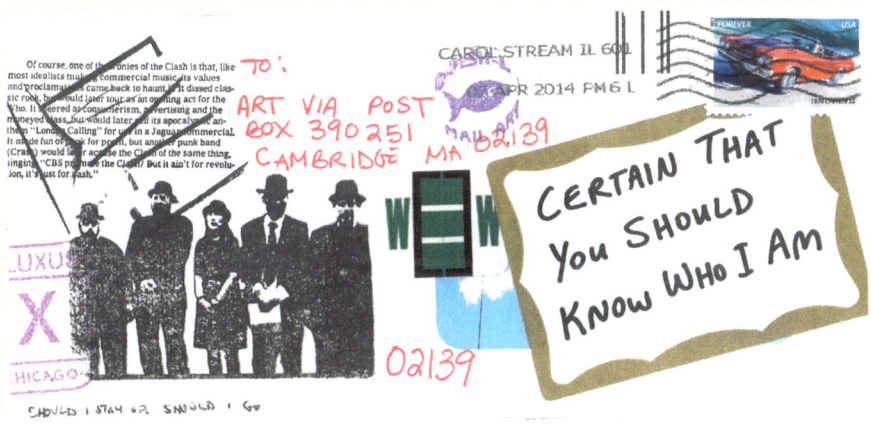

KAPSALIS, ADAMANDIA

Chicago, Illinois

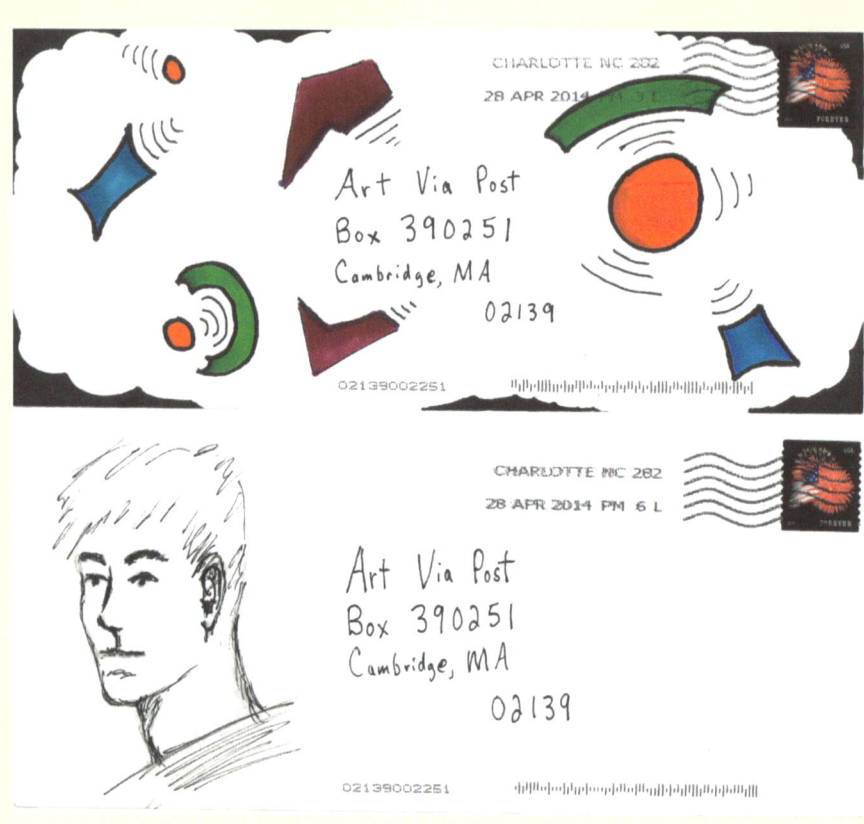

METZGAR, MATT

Charlotte, North Carolina

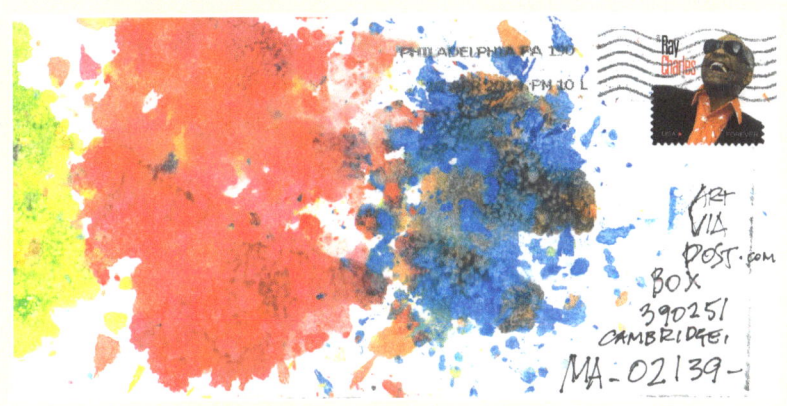

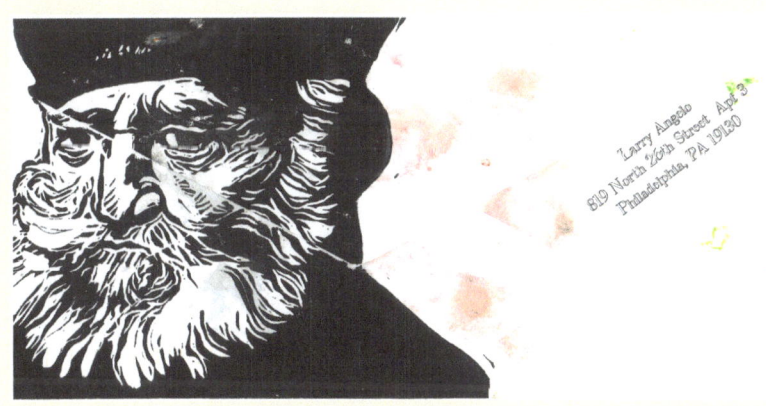

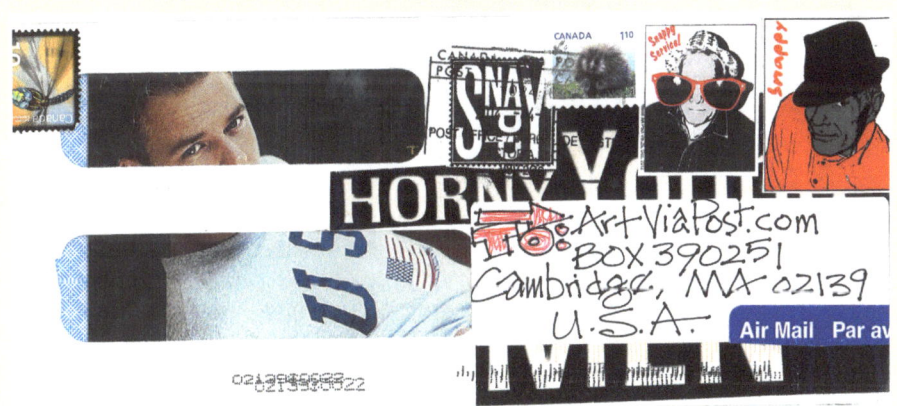

ANGELO, LARRY

Philadelphia, Pennsylvania

SNAPPY VICTORIA

Canada

snappyservice.blogspot.com

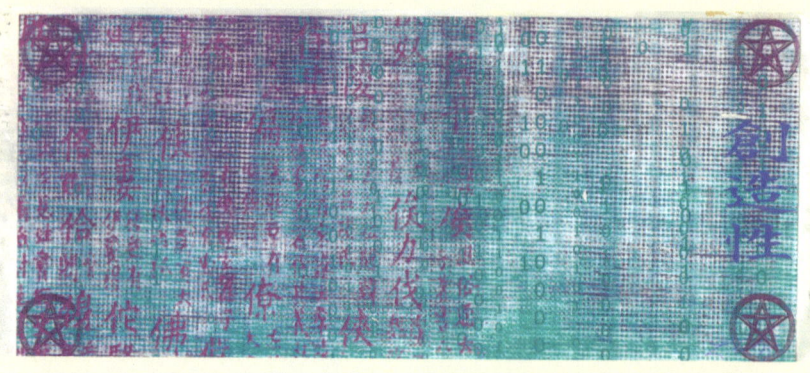

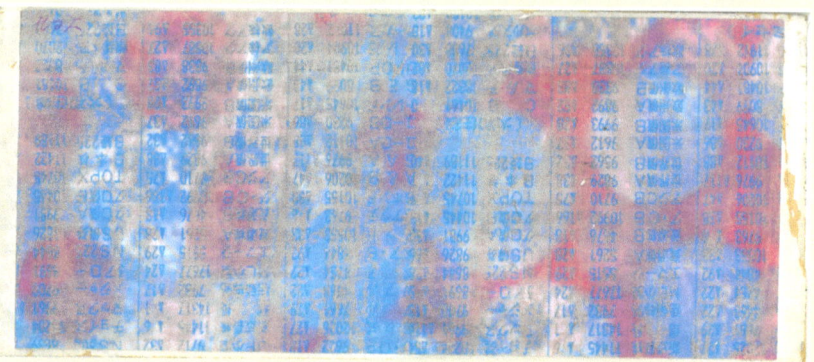

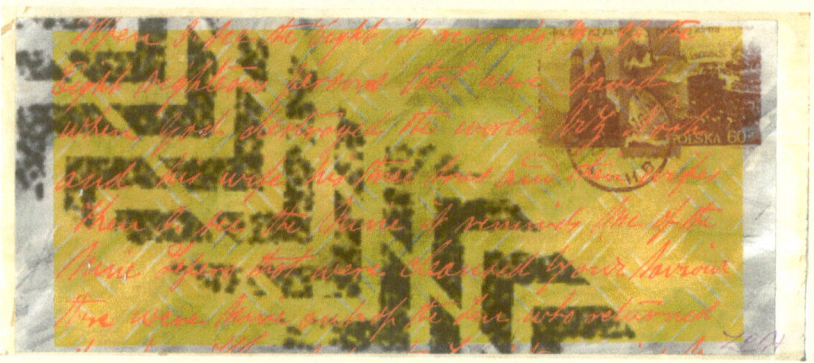

"As an artist I am always trying to push my artistic boundaries by creating something new and exciting. Submitting to Art Via Post gave me the opportunity to push my art boundaries and try something new. I love making and receiving mail art because so much about our postal system is about utilitarian function to process paperwork and bills. I want to show people that mail can be more than the monthly power bill, it can be an expression of imagination and wonder." - Laurie Hansen

HANSEN, LAURIE

Caldwell, Idaho

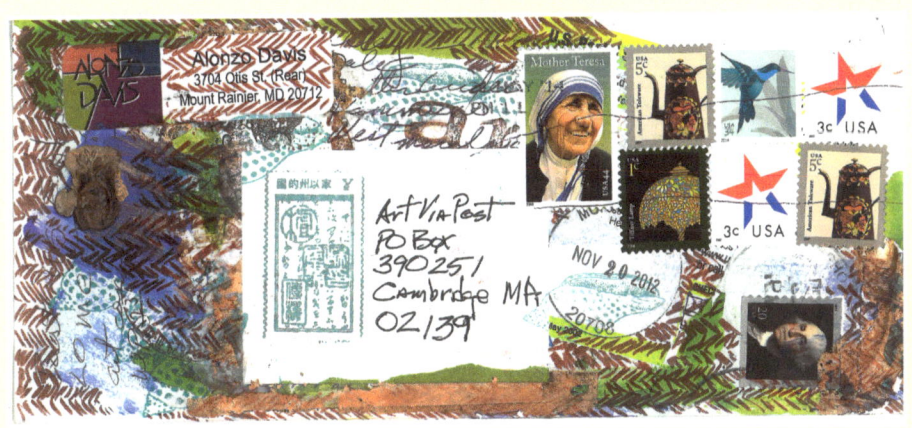

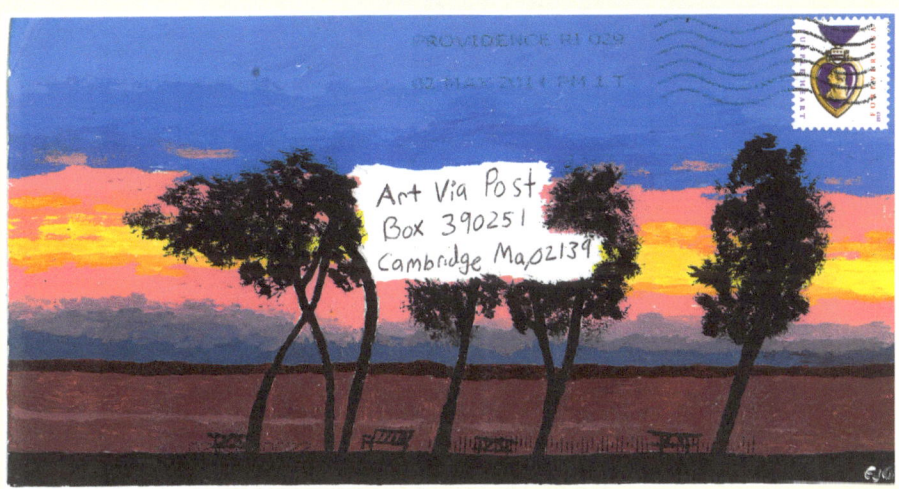

DAVIS, ALONZO

Mount Rainier, Maryland

GORG, ERIK

Riverside, Rhode Island

facebook: ArtbyErikG

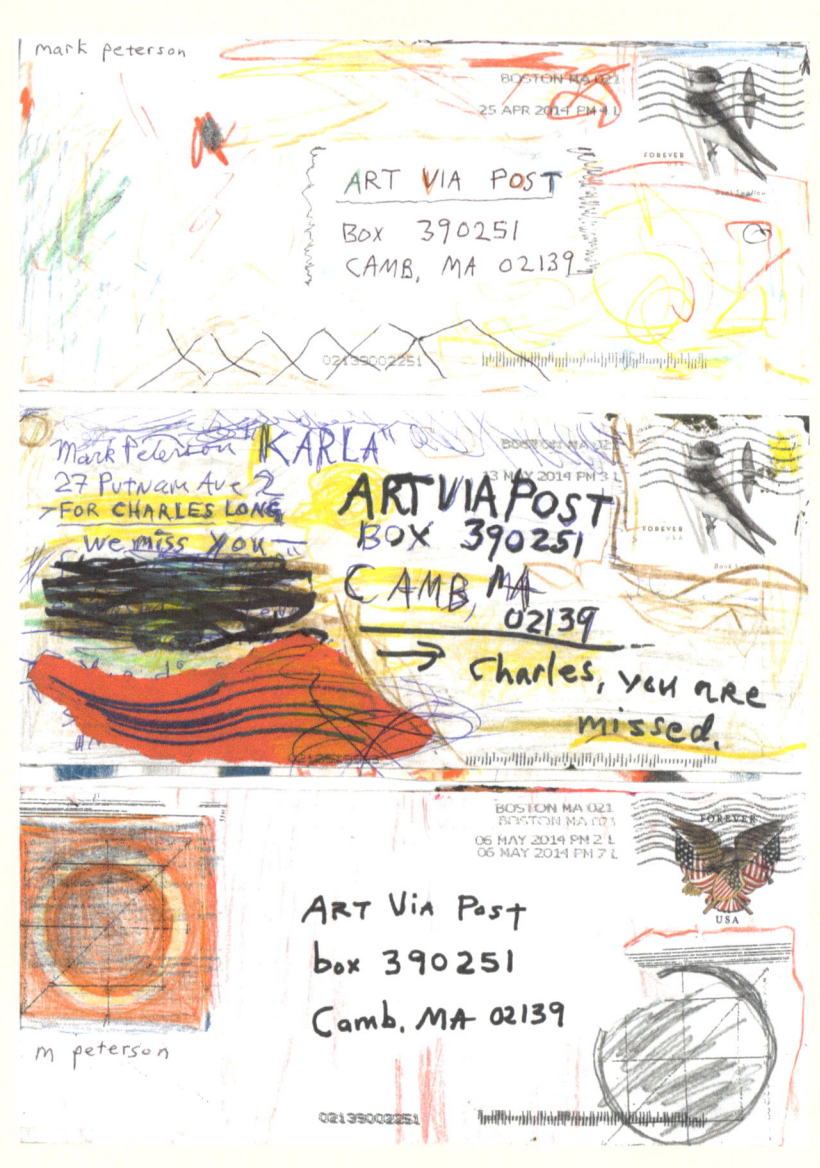

PETERSON, MARK

Cambridge, MA

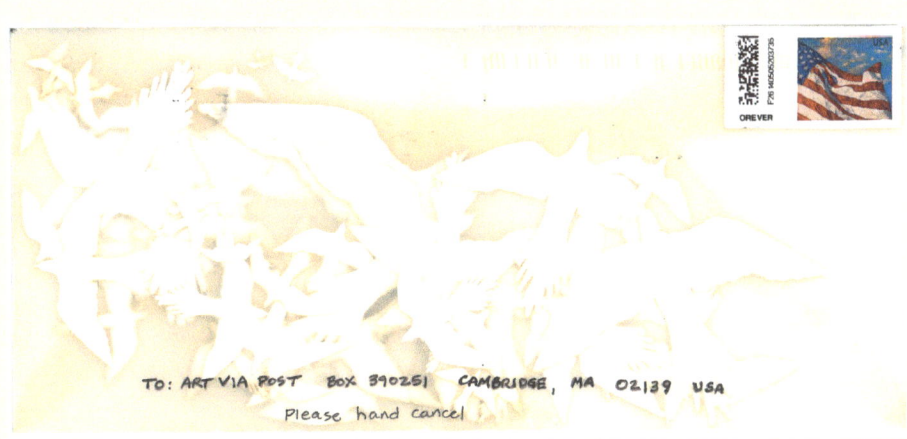

TO: ART VIA POST BOX 390251 CAMBRIDGE, MA 02139 USA

Please hand cancel

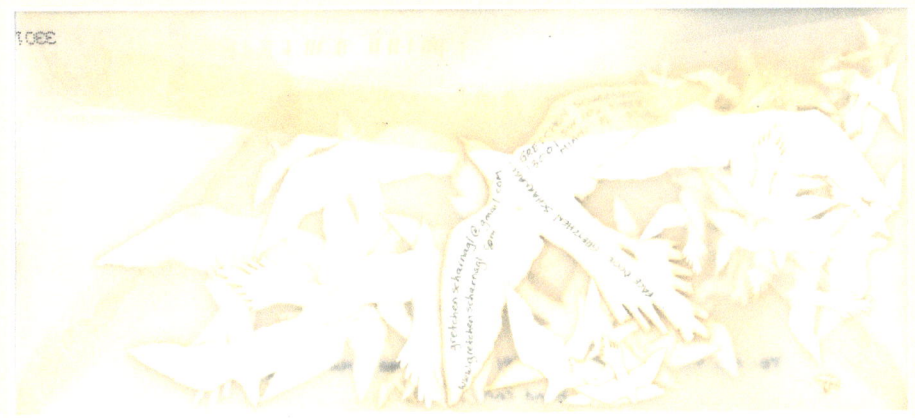

SCHARNAGL, GRETCHEN

Miami, Florida

gretchenscharnagl.com

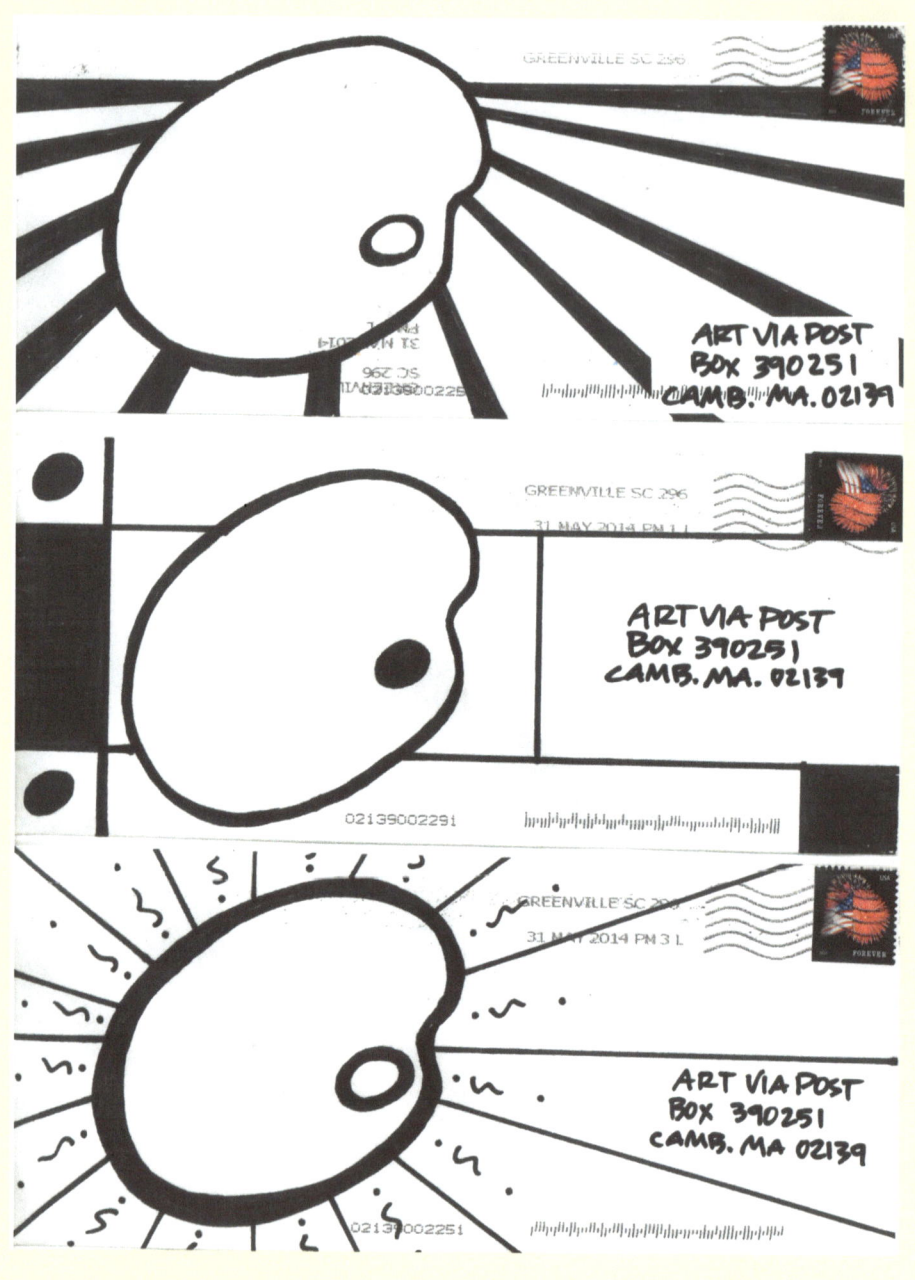

UNKNOWN

Greenville, South Carolina

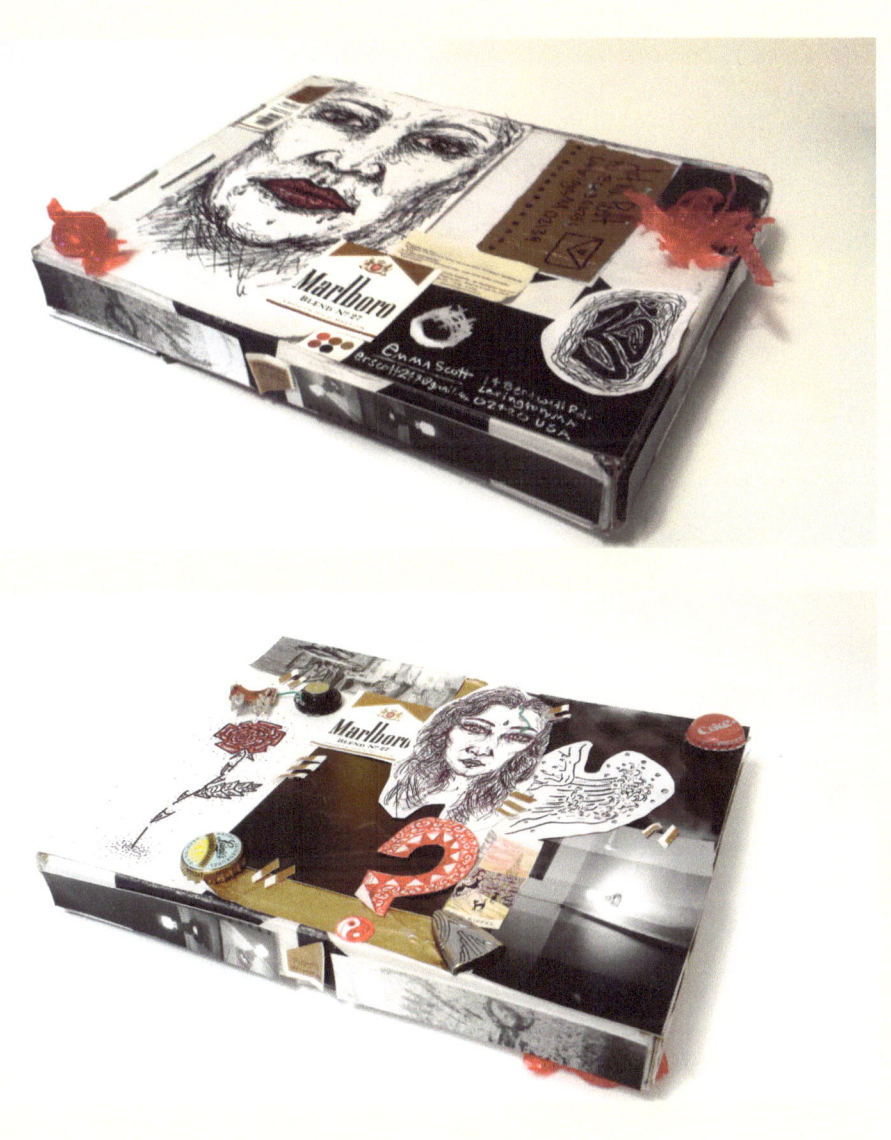

SCOTT, EMMA

Lexington, Massachusetts

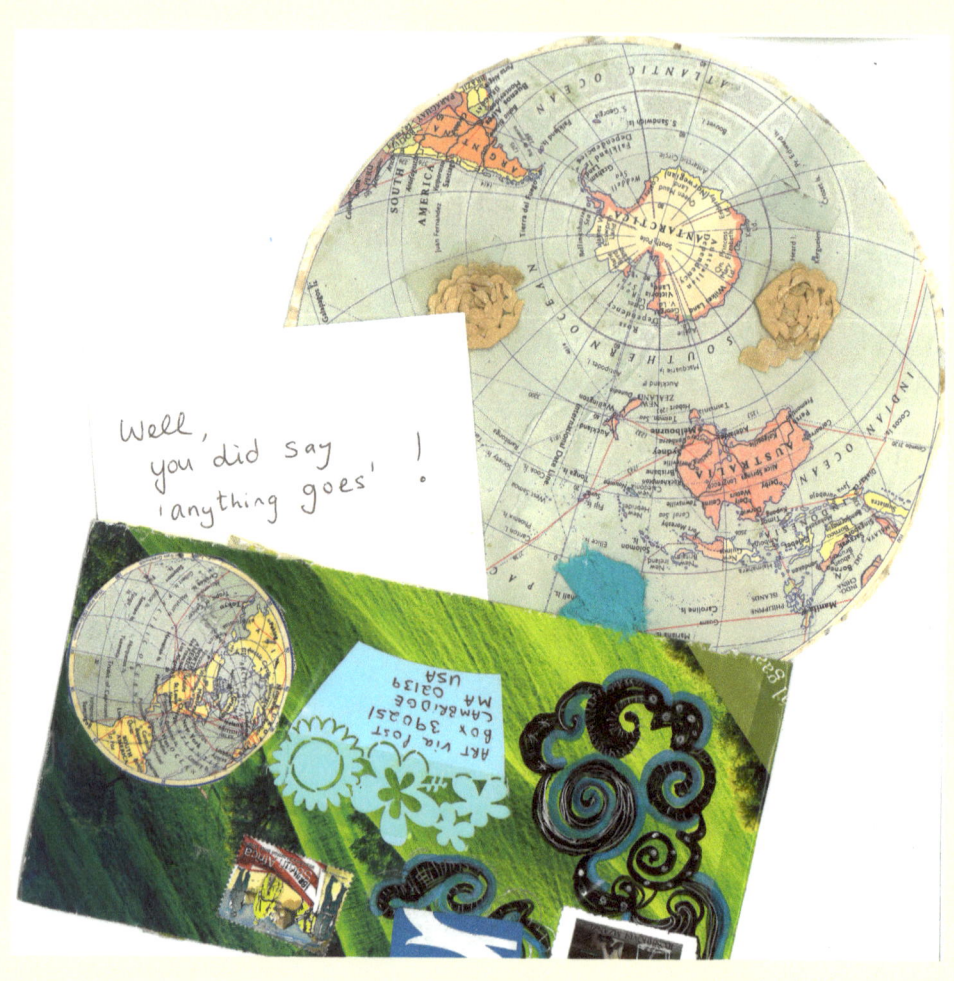

PETROL PETAL

South Africa

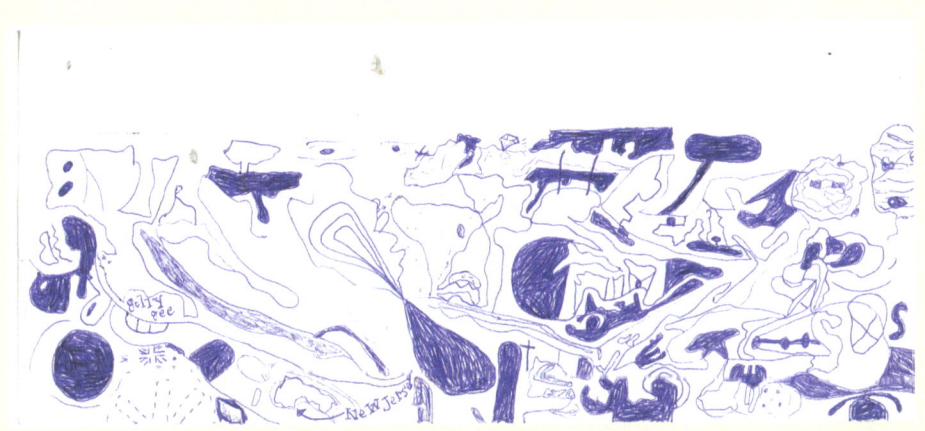

BOYER, DANIEL C.

New York, New York

www.artbreak.com/danielcboyer

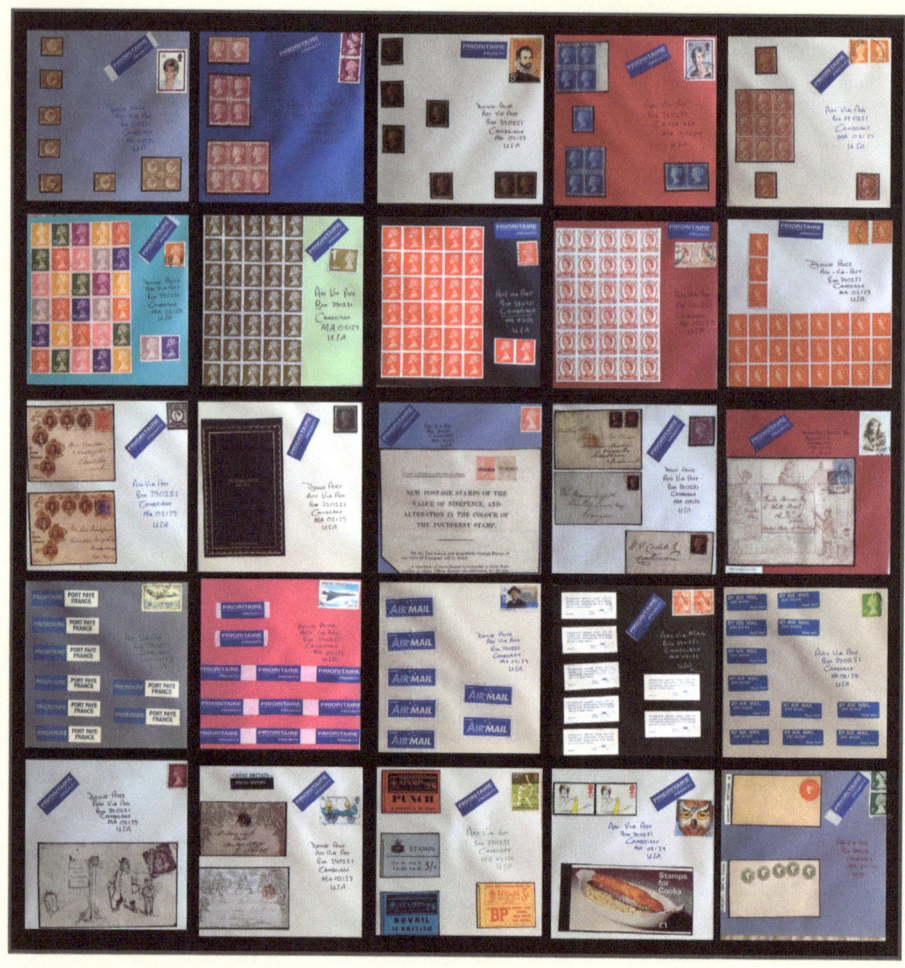

25 envelopes with historic significance fall into 5 series of 5 in each row:
Queen Victoria Stamps
Machin & Wilding Definitives
Postal History and Early Mail Art
Air Mail Labels
Postal History and Early Mail Art

- Val Herman

HERMAN, VALENTINE

France

val-herman-art.eu

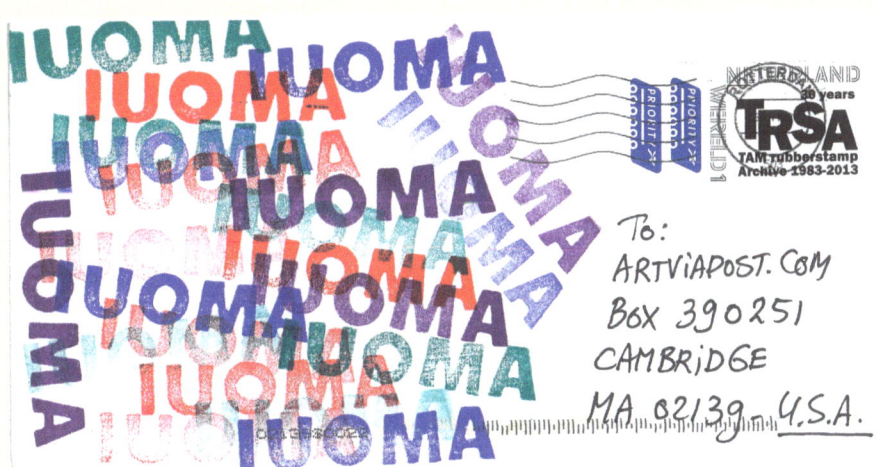

"The need to share views and ideas with others not in just a verbal way, but in a creative way. Using all the communication tools there are nowadays for the modern artist. Submitting is needed to keep the mail-art network alive and share our wiews again and again."

— Rudd Janssen

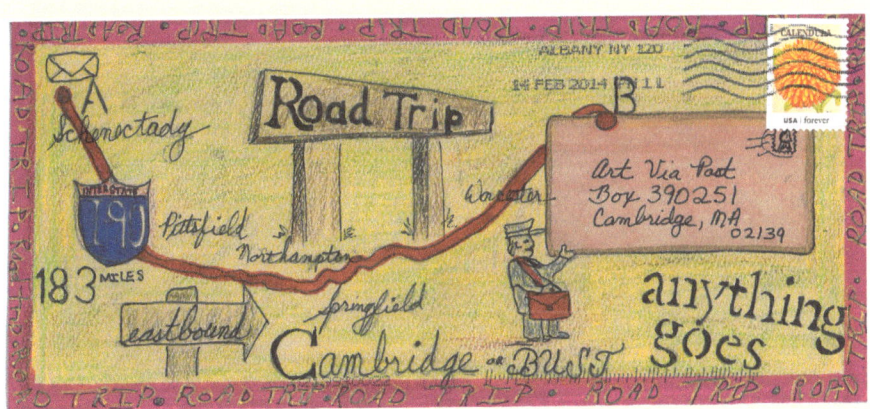

JANSSEN, RUUD

Netherlands

iiuoma.blogspot.com

VAN GENDEREN, JOANNE

Scotia, New York

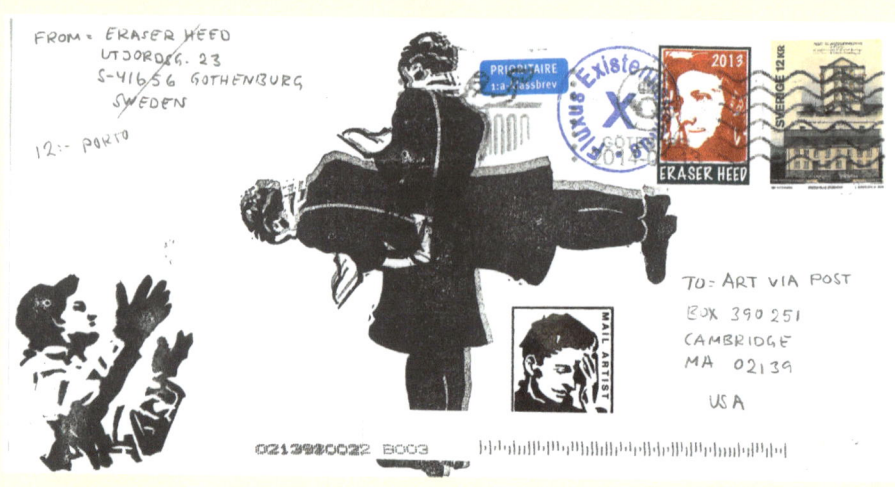

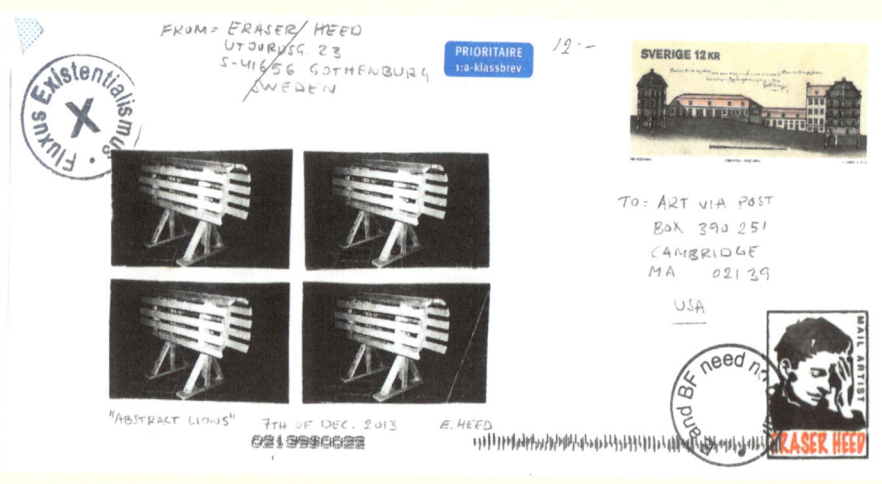

HEED, ERASER

Gothenburg, Sweeden

Facebook: Eraser Heed

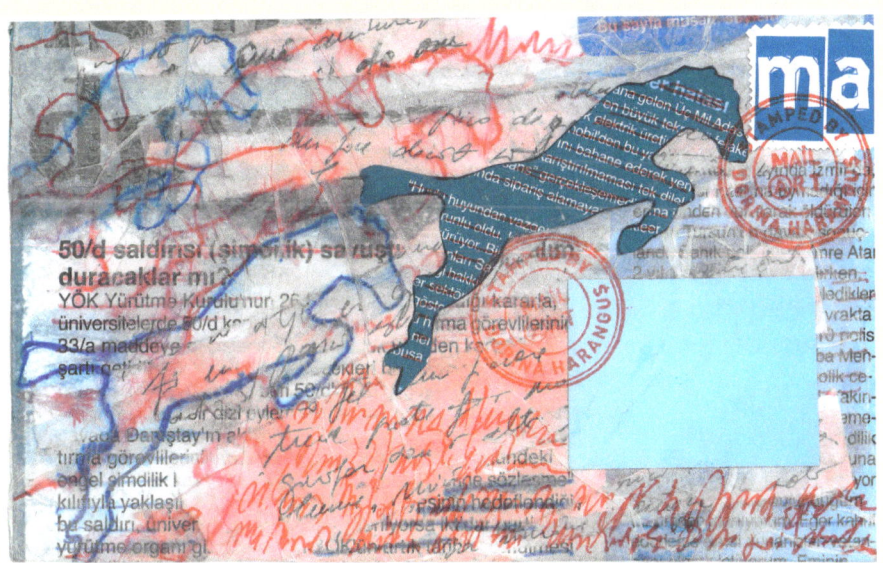

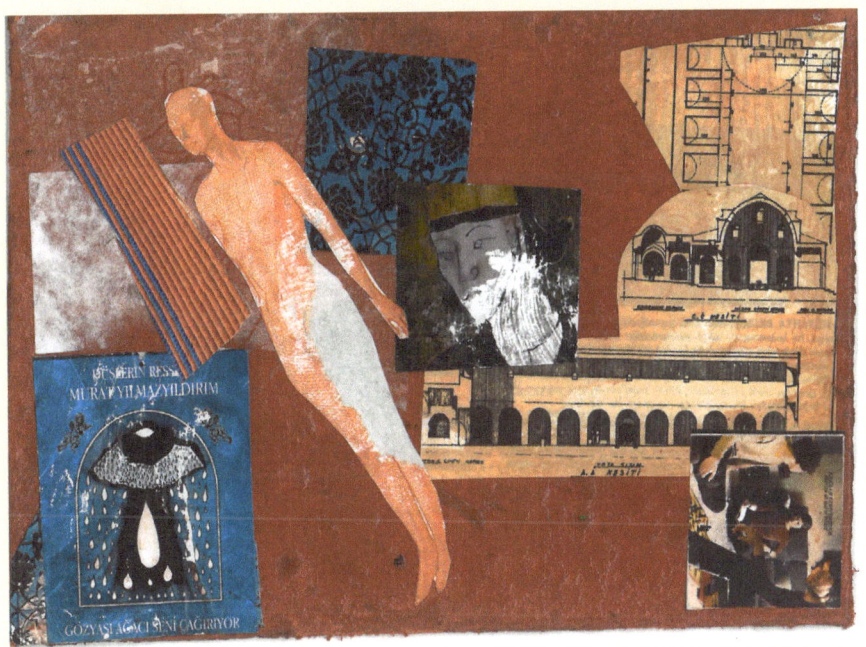

HARANGUS, DORINA

Istanbul, Turkey

ELCI, TURKAN

Istanbul, Turkey

TO: ART VIA POST
P.O. BOX 390251
Cambridge MA
02139 USA

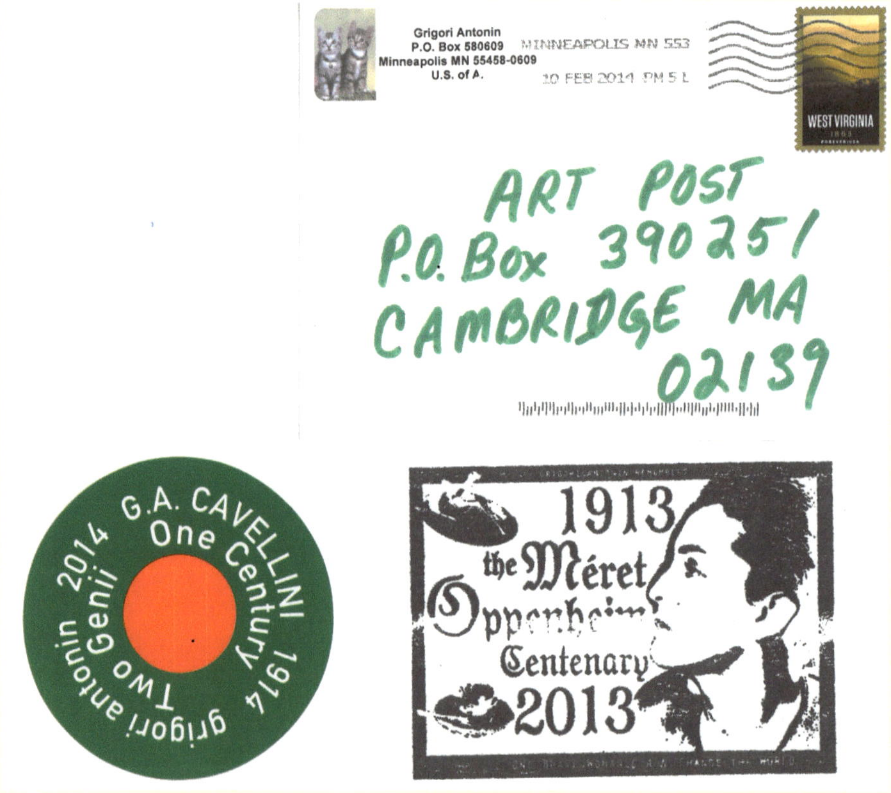

BOSTON MA 021

Grigori Antonin
P.O. Box 580609
Minneapolis MN 55458-0609
U.S. of A.

MINNEAPOLIS MN 553

10 FEB 2014 PM 5 L

WEST VIRGINIA
1863

ART POST
P.O. Box 390251
CAMBRIDGE MA
02139

2014 G.A. CAVELLINI 1914
One Century
grigori antonin Two Genii

1913
the Méret
Oppenheim
Centenary
2013

HELENA

Boston, Massachusetts

ANTONIN, GRIGORI

Minneapolis, Minnesota

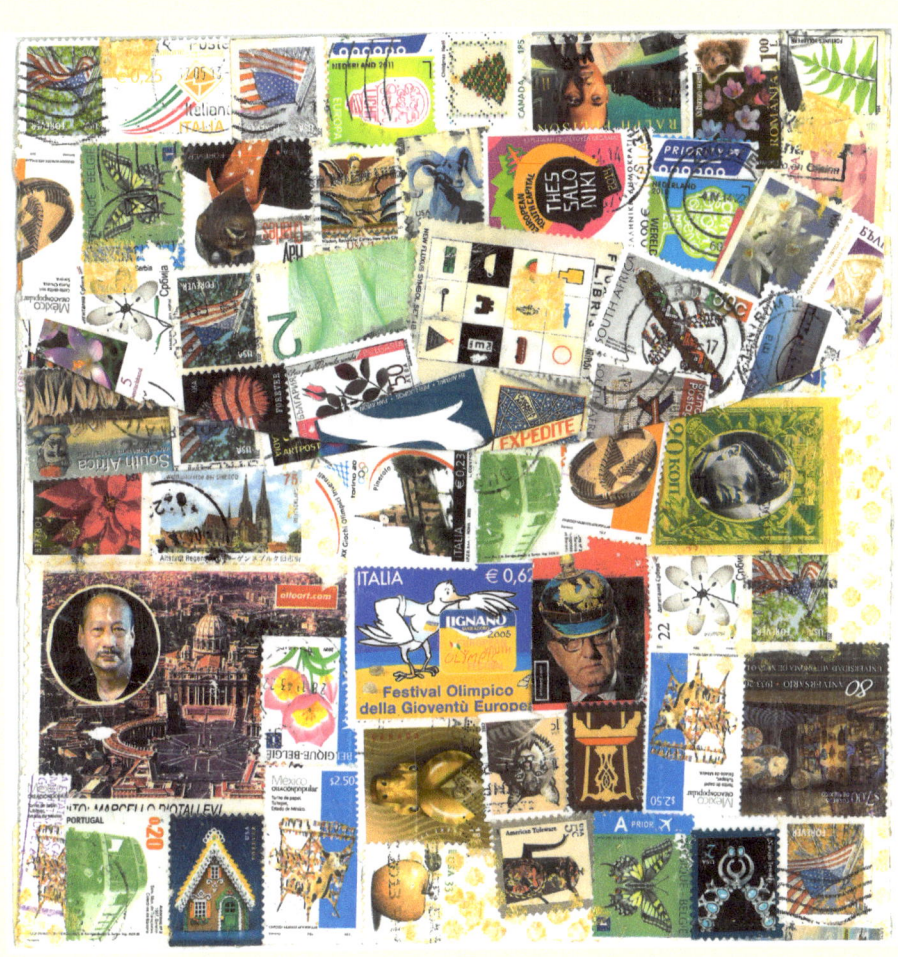

AGAR, MERAL

Istanbul, Turkey

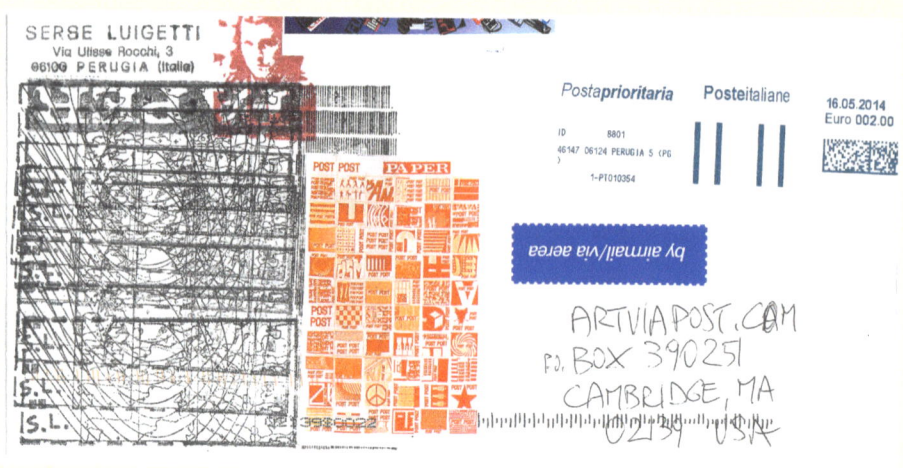

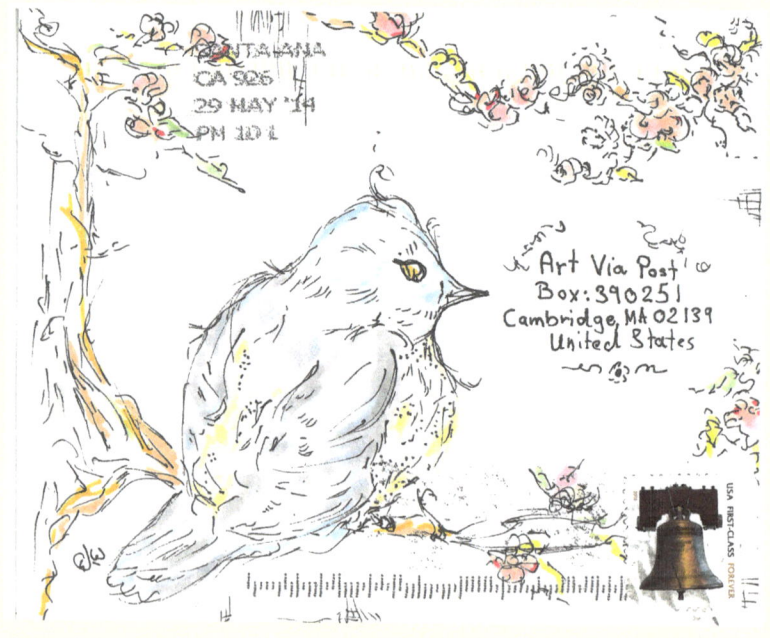

LUIGETTI, SERSE

Perugia, Italy

IDRISS, LAYAL

Santa Ana, California

layalidriss.com

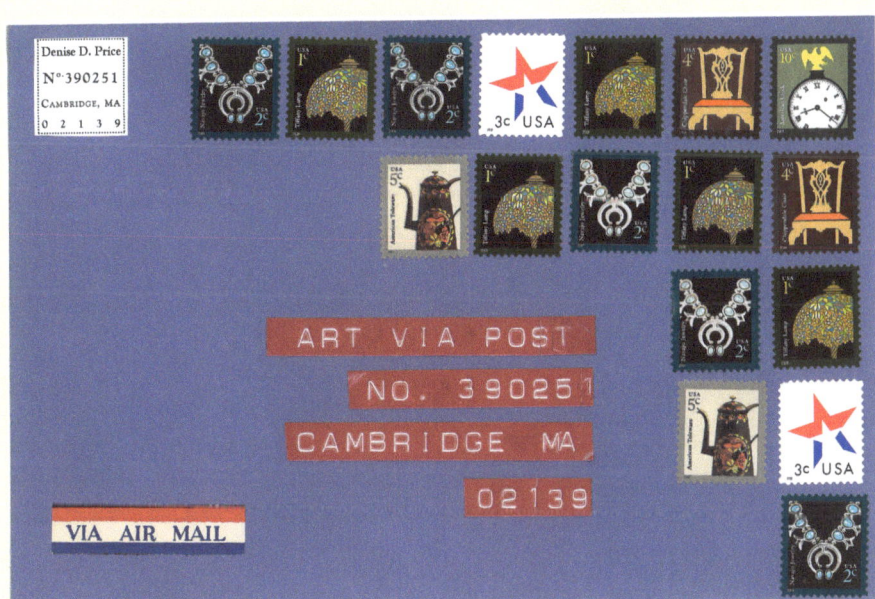

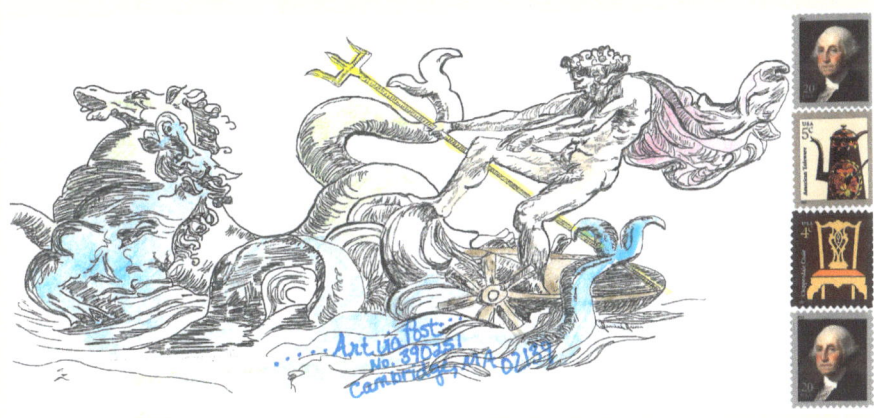

PRICE, DENISE D.

Boston, Massachusetts

denisedprice.com

instagram: denisedprice

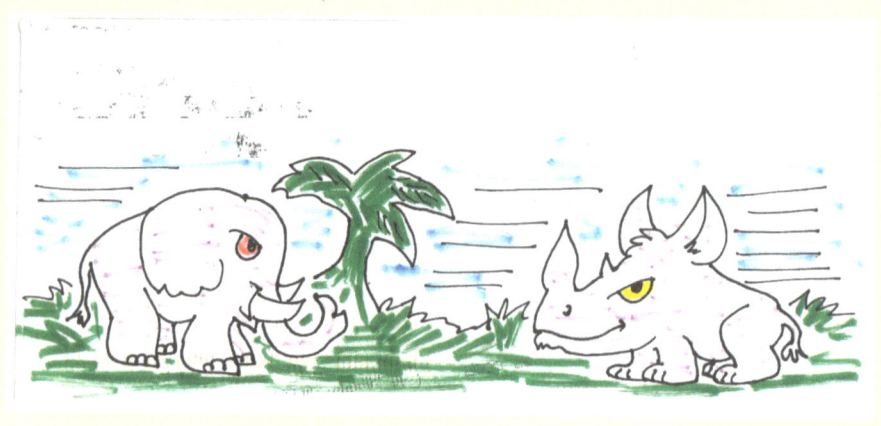

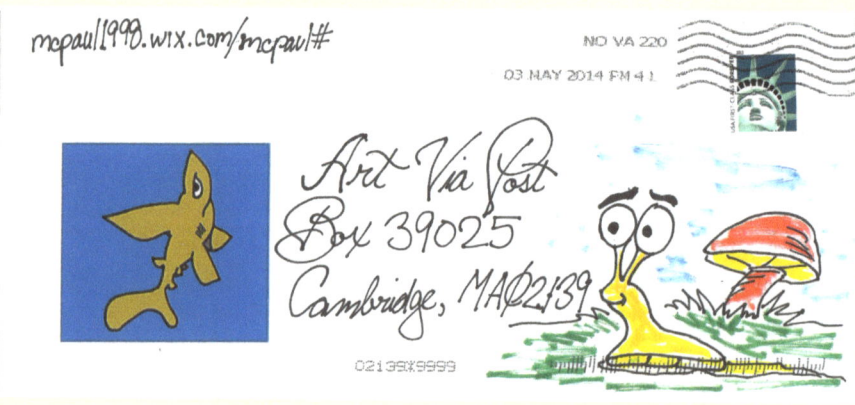

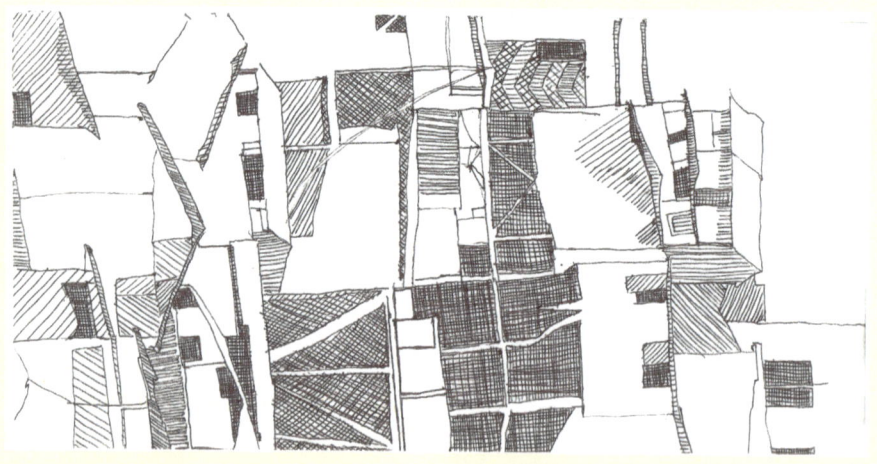

PAUL, MICHAEL C.

Arlingtn, Virginia

mcpaul1998.wix.com/mcpaul

CHASE, MEGHAN

Beverly, Massachusetts

meghanchase.com

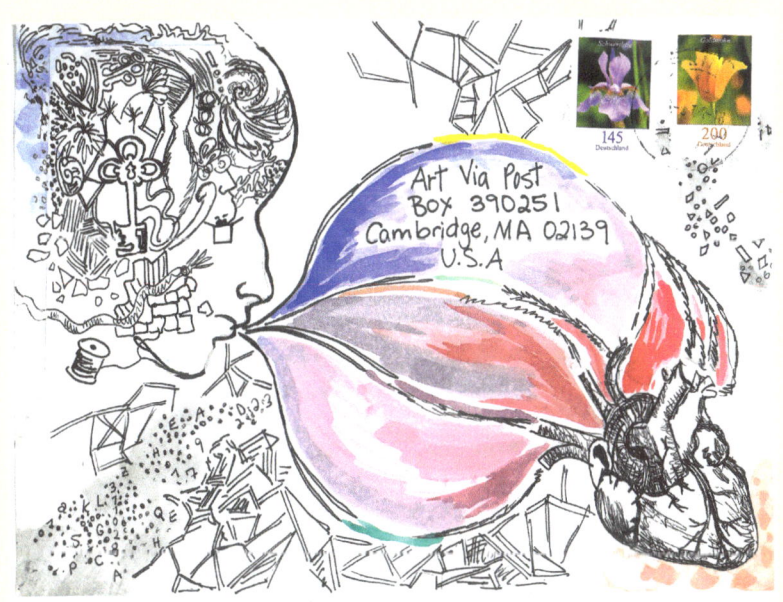

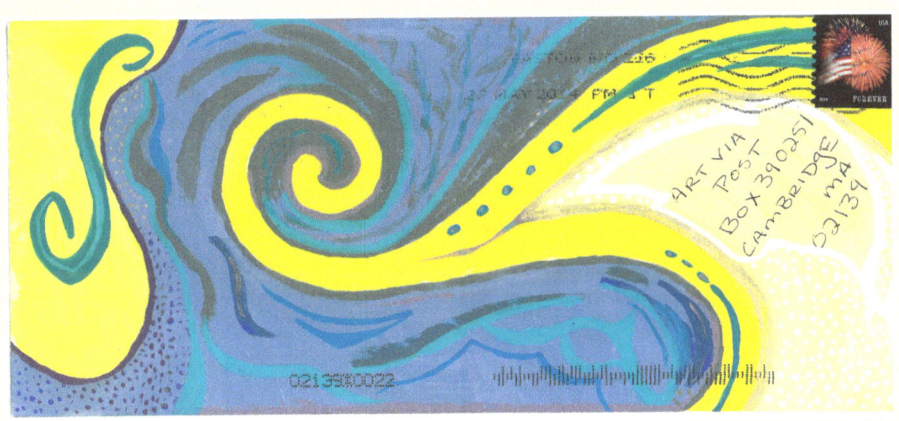

HELMES, JUJU

Germany

MOLENDA, SALLY

Salisbury, Maryland

ROGERS, INDIANA

fakefineart.tumblr.com

Instagram: indianarogers

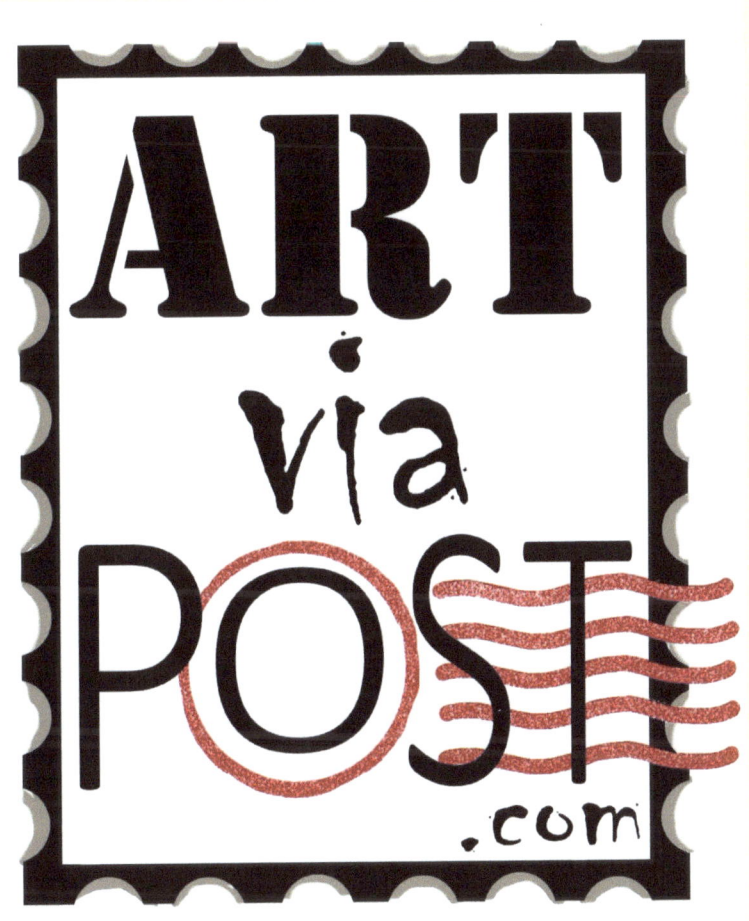

INDEX

www.ingramcontent.com/pod-product-compliance
Lightning Source LLC
Chambersburg PA
CBHW040904180526
45159CB00010BA/2921